It Is Well

IT IS WELL

— Life in the Storm —

SECOND EDITION

by
CHRIS FADDIS

Cover and interior design by Nick Heller.

ISBN:

Paperback: 978-0-692-38213-4

E-Book: 978-0-692-72784-3

Published by Chris Faddis

chris.faddis@gmail.com

Printed in the United States of America.

I dedicate this book to my children
Gianna Faustina and Augustine Valdez:

That you will read these pages one day and truly understand
the heroic nature of your mother's faith and trust in God.

That from pages of this book you will come to know
your mother's heart and the desire she had
to love and serve God with her whole being.

That you will understand from her witness
the only things that really matter in this life:
having a relationship with God,
seeking to follow His will always,
and fearlessly trusting in His promise.

I promised your mother that I would teach you
that she was resting at the heart of Jesus and to be close
to her, you would have to draw close to Him.
May you always remember this and may He be
your compass and your guide as He was
for your incredible mother.

I love you.

- Daddy

CONTENTS

Foreword

BY MARK HART

"So, what do ya think?" my (then) fiancé asked me.

The front door had not even latched yet. Angela and Chris weren't two feet out the door en route to their first "date," and already she was asking me my take on the future of their relationship. Having seen the two of them interact for all of sixty seconds I was, of course, quite thoughtful and insightful in my response.

"Honestly? I hope Chris doesn't screw it up," I replied.

I said it not because Chris was "that bad," but because Angela was that good. In the few months prior, I had gotten to know my wife's new roommate, Angela, pretty well. I had grown steadily and increasingly impressed by her. She was deep and thoughtful. She was prayerful and holy. She was healthy and invested in eating right. (Little did I know the friendship would also leave me wishing I'd invested…in organic food suppliers.) I remember saying to myself, "Chris is really gonna have to work to hang on to this one." I said this from personal experience, knowing how a good and virtuous woman can bring the very best out of a man while challenging the core of his very being. Put simply, when a woman keeps the bar high, it forces the man to ascend in character and virtue. Little did I know how prophetic that statement would become – as you'll no doubt see for yourself in the chapters that follow.

We watched as Chris courted Angela. We witnessed, first-hand, each stage of their dating journey: the late night talks, the later night disagreements, the all-day brunches, and their growth in trust, comfort and love for one another. Before long the question really wasn't a matter of whether they'd be married, but of when.

Their wedding day was beautiful, not because of the weather (it was hotter than the surface of the sun, actually) but, rather, because the "whether" was finally realized in time. The two had become one, like countless couples before them and, yet, unlike any prior. Now armed with the grace of the Sacrament, Chris and Angela would begin a new part of their journey – a journey that would require every ounce of that grace which God had now imbued them.

On the surface, their marriage looked like many others. They decorated their first apartment together. They entertained friends and family. We all went out for long dinners and laughed well into the night. They took trips and talked of future plans. In time, they had a baby girl. They moved. Started new jobs. Had another child. They did what couples do, never knowing what the future actually held for their family.

As the great Bishop Fulton Sheen once noted, "It takes three to be married." He said it because he understood something that is quickly and oft forgotten in this modern culture of self-centeredness: to become all it is intended to be by God, marriage takes three-the man, the woman and God.

There's a reason that God gives us marriage. It isn't "just" for children, although they are a beautiful fruit of it, to be sure

(Psalm 127:3). It isn't "just" to bless us out of our selfishness, although marriage assuredly invites us to grow in virtue unlike anything or anyone else on earth can do. No, scripture confirms that marriage is also how God chooses to reveal His great and unconditional love to a world and culture that has grown callous to such an indescribable reality.

Throughout the books of the Bible, there is no other analogy, no other example, no other visual God employs more to express His love for us than the love of a husband and wife. Quite literally, from Genesis to Revelation, Sacred Scripture is "book-ended" by weddings. Pope Francis reminded us all that our lives are wrapped up "in a love story" – God's love story - and when the Faddises received the news of Angela's cancer, God invited us all for a front row seat into what love truly requires: sacrifice.

During their journey with cancer, we beheld in Angela and Chris what marriages are supposed to reveal about God. We saw tenderness. We saw hope. We saw fidelity. We saw trust. We saw the kind of love that sits loyally beside a hospital bed, watching a body fade while a soul soars. Angela endured unspeakable dis-comfort as you'll read more about, but she did so with dignity and grace. Taking on the care of his bride and their beautiful children, Gianna and Augustine, Chris demonstrated the kind of sacrificial love that St. Paul talks about (Eph. 5:25) and that John Paul II her-alded as an authentic "gift of self."

Through the laughter-filled mornings, the tear-filled days and the final hours, God became the constant; the marriage was built not on two but on three, which made all the difference. As we are reminded in Ecclesiastes, "a three-ply cord is not easily broken" (Eccl. 4:12). God didn't just "hold them together," He made them

both – and all of us by extension – stronger through Angela's illness and battle.

As you read this book, you'll encounter the often harsh
reality of the Christian journey. You'll experience both the splin-
tered, bloody crucifix of Good Friday and the shiny, radiant cross
of Easter Sunday. Chris will invite you behind the closed doors into
the intimate exchanges and heaven-sent moments that should call
us all to stop and survey our own lives. Do we wake up counting
our blessings or our problems? That difference makes all the difference, as Angela demonstrated through her constant fidelity to God.

My wife, Melanie, and I stood at Angela's bedside just minutes after she went home to heaven. The room we'd been in several
times before was quite peaceful and serene. It was not a place of
death. It was a place of life; the bedroom had been transformed
into truly holy and sacred ground. During the weeks prior, the
bedside had become a place of reconciliation, thanksgiving, affir-
mation and love. In the window sat a hand-drawn picture colored
by Gianna, a rainbow of color and display of love that would rival
the finest stained glass in the most Gothic cathedral. As the light
poured through her artwork and Angela's soul had been set free,
I thanked God not only for her, but for Chris, for their children,
and for the gift of being able to witness such a journey of love until
death they did part.

Angela Faddis' story is a gift to us all, one we can and
should learn from – for her time on earth not only taught us how
to live but, more importantly, how to die. She gave us all a tutorial
on the worth of suffering, the dignity of the body and the purity of
the soul. Not merely through her words but through her example,
Angela challenged us all to trust God more. You'll see, too, that

through it all, Chris, the kids, her family and friends were beside her each step and our Father in heaven was watching over her, ushering her home to the place He'd prepared for her well in advance.

As you turn this page and the many to follow, recall and trust in the promise of God as penned through the great St. Paul:

> *"If we have died with him, we shall also live with him; if we endure, we shall also reign with him…"*
>
> (2 Timothy 2:11-12)

She ran the race. She finished victoriously. She has attained what we all desire. Until we meet again, dear Angela, please pray for us all.

Prelude

THE END BEFORE THE BEGINNING

On September 21, 2012, I held my wife's, Angela Faddis', hand for the very last time. For a little over five hours, I sat by her side, holding her hand, praying for a peaceful and a joyful entry into heaven. Her breathing had given the signal that this arduous journey of great pain was nearly over. Her heart, though still beating, was slowly giving out as was told by her pulses disappearing in the night. Still, as I held her hand, she would periodically squeeze mine as I would tell her I loved her and that she was free to go. Free to go home to her real home. Free to go with her true groom, Christ. Free to leave behind the pain, the loss, the hardship, the dreams, the hopes, the desires that filled our lives on earth, and free to enter into the complete joy and peace of heaven.

By around 7:30 am, she no longer squeezed my hand, but I held hers still. Hoping and praying she would stay long enough for our children to wake up and say goodbye. I prayed and I waited. Finally, Gianna (5) and Augustine (3) woke up and came to my side. I held them and let them know that Mommy was about to go to heaven, and it was time to say goodbye. They didn't say a lot, just slumped in my lap as they tried to make sense of it all. How many times of explaining her death would it take for them to understand what this meant? After a while, Augustine asked to go downstairs and I gave in. I asked them if they wanted to say goodbye one last time and they both declined. Augustine again insisted on going downstairs. So, I kissed Angela's head and let her know we would be coming back in a minute.

As we left the room I turned to Gianna and said, "Are you sure you don't want to say goodbye? Are you sure you don't want to kiss her one last time?" "I do want to give her a kiss but I don't want to say goodbye," she replied. With that, we returned to the room and I heard a breath that was different, final. I lifted Gianna to Angela, and she gave her a kiss. As I pulled her back, Angela took one final breath and in an instant, I knew she was gone.

We stood there as I said, "Mommy is gone." Augustine looked and laid his head on my shoulder; Gianna did the same. Holding them both in my arms as I stood above the lifeless body of my bride of only six years, I opened up the Prayers of Commendation for the Dead and asked the kids to pray. With tears and a broken voice, I spoke the prayers, and we said goodbye.

It was finished. The seventeen month journey that began with an emergency room visit which revealed a large mass in her colon and started the spiritual journey of Angela slowly surrendering to God's will was now finished on earth.

I tell you the end of this story before the beginning because it is in understanding its ending that you can fully understand what Angela and I hoped we could share with the world: despite Angela having to let go of all of her hopes and dreams for us and our family, despite losing my lover and bride, despite my children losing their mother, we believe that "it is well" because the promise of Christ remains.

I also tell you the end before the beginning for a simple yet profound reason. This life that Angela lived, while cut short in our eyes, is only the beginning. Angela's death was indeed not the end for her. The promise of heaven awaited her once she left this life and that curtain closed. It is an end for us who are left behind, but it is a beginning for those who are faithful, for those who trust and believe in God. Indeed, Angela's life on this earth was but a prelude to the life of eternal joy in heaven.

At her funeral our personal friend and Angela's confessor in those last days of her life, Father John Parks, shared a bit of insight from his meetings with Angela:

> "At the same meeting, the same meeting when Angela shared with me her heart, that her one real desire since she'd been an adult was that she would just raise a beautiful, Catholic family, at that same meeting she says, 'You know, I have this dream that I'm close to death, and I'm in great suffering, and Chris, my husband, is holding me, and he's holding me tight, and then suddenly he begins to fade away. Chris begins to slip away, and he's replaced, and now Jesus is holding me, and I'm no longer suffering because I'm home.'"

Father Parks had not shared this story with me personally, so the first time I heard it was in his homily at Angela's funeral. I was overcome with emotion as he shared what had transpired, because as I sat holding Angela's hand that morning, I could feel her fade away. In those final moments, Jesus certainly held her as she waited for the children to say goodbye.

Indeed, this story I tell in these pages is a story of pain, suffering, despair, tragedy, fear, worry, hardship and death. Yet, it is so much more. This story I have to tell is the story of how God, in His goodness and mercy can make straight the crooked and painful path of life. This story is God's story in our lives. This story is how joy can be found in the midst of suffering and how death is not the end. Life on this earth and our ultimate death are but a prelude, they are the opening score. On the other side of that curtain lies a promise that is greater than anything you or I can ever dream of on this earth.

I pray that in the pages of this book, I can faithfully and adequately share the gift God has given us in this great burden. I share this burden because I believe God calls us to be a good steward of all we are given. If we are given a heap of money or a heap of manure, the response God expects from us is the same: faithfulness.

Friendship, Love, and the In-Betweens

THROWING A BRIDGE

As Mass was about to begin, I was looking for a seat in my normal section when suddenly a woman with silky brown hair and an amazing smile caught my attention, forcing me to stop in my tracks. She was wearing a turquoise top and white pants, and she was simply stunning. "Were her eyes blue? Or green?" I thought, as she passed by me. I found my place and kept my eyes peeled for her to pass by again. Who was this girl? Where did she come from? I would not find out immediately, but I kept my eyes peeled for her each week, and eventually we met by chance at a restaurant where she was eating with a mutual friend. Her name was Angela, and there was just something about her that I could not get out of my head. Over the next few months we'd get to know each other slowly as we went out weekly with a large group of young adults from the parish. Perhaps by chance or maybe it was on purpose, we would constantly find ourselves sitting together or walking together or riding together. As we grew ever closer together, I would learn a little more about her each week. I found myself wanting to see her more and more.

It was a few months before she accidentally asked me on a date to see Cirque de Soleil. Though she wasn't so sure she was thinking of romance, I had made up my mind. It reminds me of Blessed John Paul II's play, The Jewelers Shop, where we learn the story of Andrew and Teresa, two young lovers who get engaged. Andrew speaks of Teresa in this way: "Teresa was a whole world, just as distant as any other man, as any other woman – and yet there was something that allowed one to think of throwing a bridge." The more time I spent with Angela, the more intrigued I was and the more I would want to know about this "other world," and so I had made up my mind that I would throw a bridge. We would spend quite a bit of time together over the course of a month, beginning with that "accidental" date. I was clear that while I valued our friendship, my intention was to date her and pursue her heart. She would repeatedly let me know that she wasn't looking to date, but it sure seemed like the opposite to me and to those around us. I continued to pursue her heart. One day after spending an afternoon of picnicking, she finally said, "I guess we're dating." To which I replied, "Is that a good thing?" She said yes. It seemed only fitting at this point to kiss, and I can say without a doubt that it was by far the worst first kiss in history. It was so awkward that we both laughed about it a few minutes later. But that kiss did not ruin anything. Love had begun to be forged within. Angela's hesitancy to date was a true blessing in that it forced me to get to know her heart.

Our courtship was marked with incredible friendship and intense prayer. We hiked together, cooked together, worked out together, explored together, read together, and we became best friends. As our hearts grew into one, it was clear that we were meant to marry. Knowing this was the desire of each of our hearts, we took our time to continue to discern. As we neared the time I had hoped to ask her to marry me, we faced some real challenges in our relationship. We went on a mission trip to Mexico, and it challenged us both individually and in our love for one another. Over the month following that trip, we would have to decide if we were going to love each other even in the hard parts of life. One night after a long and heated argument, Angela looked me in the eyes and said very intently, "You have to trust that I only have good in mind for you, and I would never do anything to intentionally hurt you. You have to trust that I love you, and I only want good for you."

In her words I had to face a very real fact. I not only didn't trust in her love for me, but I also didn't trust in God's love for me. We had spent a lot of time talking about "trust" of God together. Her words that night made me face the fact that I did not trust that I was worthy of her love, God's love or anyone else's love for that matter. Angela, too, had to face similar doubts and fears. I recall Angela saying at one point, "We need to decide now if we are going to see this through, because if I walk out that door, I will not be coming back. You have to decide if you trust me to love you, and I have to decide the same." That night we both had to choose to love in the midst of doubt, fear, past hurts and the like, but we also had to choose to trust that God had our best intentions in mind. Even in our courtship, I can hear clearly the voice of the Father calling, speaking, telling me to trust in Him. I knew then that Angela was the woman I was supposed to marry and that she would lead me to heaven without a doubt.

Just over a month later, on her birthday, I would take

Angela on an adventure. I told her I was taking her to brunch in Fountain Hills, Arizona. We had many of our early dates in Fountain Hills, and it was a special place for Angela. As we neared the place where we would have brunch, I handed her a blindfold and asked her to put it on. I made a detour and instead of going to the resort, I pulled up to Fountain Hills Park where a 100-foot fountain would be the backdrop for my proposal. I walked her out to the grass and told her to count to thirty before taking off the blindfold. It was Angela's birthday and also the Feast of St. Therese of Lisieux who was her favorite saint, so I left a trail of roses each with a note. I then ran ahead to where friends had placed a blanket and a dozen roses, and there I waited for her. As she approached, I dropped to one knee and asked her to be my life's companion. Being the Feast of St. Therese I asked her if we could dedicate our engagement to St. Therese. We were married nine months later on July 1, 2006 at St. Mary's Basilica in Phoenix.

I won't say our marriage was perfect. I don't believe there is such a thing. I recall a friend telling me once that he wasn't sure if he was ready to ask his girlfriend of two years to marry him yet because he wasn't worthy or holy enough for her. I reminded him that if he was perfect, he wouldn't need her; maybe their marriage is what would help him to become a better man. Angela and I were certainly works-in-progress, and there was lots of work to be done in each of us. In marriage you certainly see the best and worst in another person. The hidden parts are hard to hide when you join your lives into one. However, it is incredible when someone sees your "ugly side" and still chooses to love you. I often hear people comment on their spouse's ugly side with a statement of "I didn't sign up for this." Angela and I learned very quickly of the "ugly side" but by the grace of God, we also knew in our hearts that we signed up for all of it. This lived trust that we shared in our marriage to one another taught each of us a lot about God's love and a lot about what it means to trust in him. We both had to trust one another with our mutual "ugly sides" and we had to trust that God had a plan for our marriage, and for each of us.

A week after Angela's death, I found a letter she had written to me three months before we were to be married. In it she wrote,

> *I really feel that God is setting us up to do great things for Him. That's a lot of pressure, but I know that through lots of prayer and submission to His will, we could be the first married saints. HaHa! I'm sort of kidding, cause the recognition isn't important, but I know we've talked about this before, and I hope at least our kids will think it's true. I'm so glad my vocation is marriage so I can pursue sainthood with you.*

In hindsight I can see His hand and hear His voice in our lives leading up to Angela's cancer diagnosis. Looking back at our life together, I can see that God was preparing our hearts for this all along. God, in His loving kindness, was gently leading us on this journey in a way that would prepare us to trust Him completely with our lives, even unto death. God's firm placement of a desire to trust Him so fully with our hearts is, in and of itself, a true gift. As Angela neared death, so many things that she had encountered in her life and that we had encountered in our short time together began to make sense. In many ways, some of those hardships she had faced even before cancer seemed to be redeemed during her final suffering.

As the world watched Angela willfully surrender to God's will at the end of her life, I believe it became very clear to all of us that Angela's "submission to His will" was heroic. To look back at her words to me and see this clear desire in her heart for holiness and sainthood is a great gift. I can see that while our plans for life may not have worked out the way we would have desired, God clearly called Angela to this surrender and this witness long before she was diagnosed with cancer. Cancer was not the instigator of this journey; cancer was merely a means to an end.

SUFFERING AND TRUST

Angela's journey through life was not an easy one. She suffered from depression and anxiety. Early on in our relationship, I would begin to see this suffering that she endured, and we would talk frequently about trust, worry, and her desire to be able to trust God with her whole heart. She never struggled to believe that God was good and that He was trustworthy; her struggle was with believing she was worth God's love. She struggled with a great deal of worry that she was making bad decisions. She also struggled with a very difficult relationship in her life that continually caused her pain. Still, Angela's desire to trust in God led her to turn this depression, worry, anxiety and difficult relationship over to Him.

The depression was not constant. She would have phases where she would have difficult days or weeks, but for the most part, her depression was manageable. However, after we moved back east and ended up in North Carolina, Angela's depression returned with a vengeance. For the better part of two years, Angela dealt with severe depression. While our marriage actually thrived through this time, her personal struggles were very difficult. There were days when Angela and I both felt helpless. The only thing that got us through was praying the Divine Mercy Chaplet. Even when she didn't feel like praying or when she was most in despair, she would ask me to pray the words for her. There were times when she would be so angry throughout the prayer, and then at the very end, as we recited the powerful words, "Holy God, Holy Mighty one, Holy Immortal One, have mercy on us and on the whole world," Angela's disposition would almost instantly change. She would later tell me that there were times when I was praying the words for her that she would be so angry at how she felt that she'd want to scream, but every time we got to that part of the prayer, it would all go away. I was constantly amazed at how even when she couldn't "feel" God's love, she would say to me, "I can't feel God's love. What I feel is hate and sadness, but I know He loves me and I trust He loves me even though I don't feel it." From the very beginning of our relationship, trust was a major theme because of both my call to speak and write on the topic of trust and also Angela's desire and struggle to trust. We would bond on this topic early on and dedicate our relationship to leading each other to trusting in God in all things.

Shortly after Gianna was born, we made the decision to move so I could attend chiropractic school. After a short stay with Angela's family in the D.C. area, we moved to Atlanta, Georgia, where I was going to work for a year while finishing up some pre-requisites and then begin school. While in Atlanta, the job I had hoped for fell through, and the money we had saved up began to run out. I looked for work everywhere I could. I was barely able to keep enough money coming in to pay for basic needs. During that time we would attend Mass daily (sometimes twice a day), pray unceasingly, and did everything in our power to find a way out.

As things began to get grim, we took our friend up on an offer to stay at a camp north of Atlanta and take some time to really pray through what God desired for us. During that stay Angela found a book that was left in our cabin called *God Alone Suffices* by Slawomir Biela. I recall Angela saying she didn't want to read it. At one point in a moment of lament, she said, "I'm done talking about trusting God. We've trusted and look where we are." As I continued to look for work during this time, I would often walk to the chapel and pray. A big part of my prayer was that God would help us to trust again. One afternoon, after I had been gone for a few hours, I came back to the cabin. Angela was in tears but had a smile on her face. She began to tell me all about this book. She said we had to trust that God would provide; we had to live the way we always said we wanted to, and we had to let Him take control. She then shared the book with me, and pointed out some of the specific quotes. That day we rededicated our marriage to a complete trust in God's will. Within a few days I had two job interviews and a week or so later, I was in Winston-Salem, North Carolina where I was offered a job. We learned a lot through that experience, and this new resolve to trust carried us through what would be a blessed but difficult time in North Carolina.

While our marriage thrived, we struggled to feel at home in North Carolina, despite having some wonderful friends and a great parish. Financially, we were barely making it due to my low salary as a parish youth minister. That same relationship that had been a great trial for Angela continued to cause great pain and even estrangement from Angela's family. As I mentioned above, Angela's depression worsened greatly. Still, she continued to trust even on her most difficult days of depression. The shared disposition to rely on God had settled deep within and prepared us to handle anything.

After many attempts at counseling and discussions about seeking more serious help, we finally decided to take Angela to see a naturopathic medical doctor. After that initial visit, it was clear to the naturopath that Angela had sure signs of a disorder called reactive hypoglycemia, which basically caused a sugar spike that would lead to anxiety and depression. She suggested that Angela start with some basic diet changes to see if it would help. Within two days we saw an immediate change. Angela felt good, had energy, and was no longer having anxiety attacks throughout the day. Three or four days into this, we stopped in the hallway, and we both cried tears of joy. She was herself again. Those next three months were incredible. It was like a honeymoon all over again, and Angela was beginning to feel in control of her emotions and life. I can't tell you how many times we thanked God for this burden finally being lifted.

PRELUDE TO CHANGE

There are days and even seasons in life that begin with a dull ache before the crash of a great pain. We often cannot decipher the dull ache until the pain hits. Something seems a little bit off or not quite right. It can come as a feeling of discontent, disconnectedness, or the uneasy feeling in the gut that makes one wonder what is wrong. In the days and weeks leading up to April 24, 2011,

I did not quite know that something difficult was about to happen, but the winds of change were blowing and what seemed so certain for the coming months was beginning to be unclear. Still, I could not have known that this dull ache that was welling in my soul was leading to something of such significant impact.

As Good Friday approached, I had been swamped with work and feeling a little anxious about life. Something, as I said above, seemed a little off. Having to work on Good Friday, I didn't quite know yet if I would make it to any Good Friday services, so I decided to at least attend a weekly prayer breakfast I had been invited to a few times previously. A local pastor spoke and while I don't remember all of what he said, one thing stood out. He spoke about how we constantly "vow" in our lives. We make promises to do things or to never do things again. We promise to make things right or better. In his view the bottom line was that it is God's vow to us that matters. His covenant with us, His promise to us, His dying on the Cross for us is the only vow we need.

His words struck a chord with me because in the weeks and months leading up to this day, I had made many vows to myself and to Angela. I vowed that we would never be poor again, that I would never let our family suffer the kind of trials we had suffered in the past, and that I was going to make a life for us. As I'll share in later parts of this book, we had been through an awful lot of struggle in our lives to this point. Only in the few months leading up to this day had we begun to see the light as things improved financially and otherwise.

I went straight home instead of going to work, and I told Angela about the talk and said, "I am not going to vow to change our lives anymore. I'm going to trust and be a good steward of what God has given us and of our family." It truly was a moment of spiritual freedom for me. That was Good Friday. Little did I know that exactly 48 hours later, Resurrection Sunday, doctors would call me in to the emergency room where our lives would be changed forever.

Storm

The waves crashed the sides of the boat like the strike of a wrecking ball, tossing the boat this way and that. The lightning struck all around, so much that the night sky became bright as day. The rain came down in sheets giving no relief. Had one woken in the night, they would have wondered if they were in the sea. It seemed there was no end in sight. This storm will not give way, the passengers in tow wondered if they would see the light of another day. With each pounding of thunder, the heart grew with anxiety. Water sloshed about the deck and worry began to mount that the ship and all on board would sink. As worry grew, the mind began to think of the worst outcome and despair set in. Could this possibly end, could any be saved?

"With that they cried out, 'Master, Master, we are perishing.' He awakened, rebuked the wind and the waves, and they subsided and there was calm"

(Luke 8:24)

THE GREATEST STORM OF OUR LIVES BEGINS

I still hear the ringing in my ears as I think of that morning. The deafening words spoken by the young doctor, as he stuttered and struggled to tell us the news, still brings me to my knees. "The CT scan shows a large mass in your colon," he said. His shaken voice told me more than his actual words. "It is appearing to cause a complete blockage, and we also see some spots on your liver and possibly your ovary." The senior doctor at his side looked rattled too, but with more calm, he gave mercy to the young resident. "We cannot confirm a diagnosis without a biopsy, but it appears to be colon cancer and given the spread, it is very advanced; we will have a surgical team in here in a few minutes to discuss your options, but it will need to be addressed quickly." With that, they left the room.

Just like that, our lives, at least our vision of our lives and all that we assumed was assured, crashed to the floor. Our love, our family, our hopes for our future, our desires and dreams all of them no longer in our hands. Shattered pieces of glass, the only sign left of what we once knew for certain, all of it, in a million pieces. Frozen in time is that moment. Scattered in time are those dreams. The ringing. The glass. A million pieces.

What do you say when your lover lies in a bed, hearing the same words as you, knowing what it means, what it all likely means? Death. End. Loss. Words, they come easy for me. But not now. Not in this moment. I try. I attempt to muster some sort of comfort, but the words, they don't come. She, the one who has a hard time with words, the one who needs the comfort in this moment, she says the words, the only words that matter: "Jesus still rose, so we will trust." Shattered hopes, shattered dreams, a shattered life, and she says the only thing that matters in this life. Jesus still rose.

RESURRECTION DAY

It was Easter Sunday. It was a day we had looked forward to for weeks. Angela, having come through this horrible period of depression, felt that Lent was her new beginning. We were so excited for what Easter joy would bring.

Angela had been sick for several days. She was constipated and nothing seemed to work. We had seen her doctor who gave her a list of different things to try. At one point things had seemed to improve and Angela was feeling great, but then Friday came and the pressure and nausea was intense. We called her doctor again who gave us a couple more things to try and then said, "If this doesn't work by tomorrow, you need to go into the ER." Saturday came and no relief. I had to work, and Angela was miserable with pain, nausea and all over discomfort.

That evening I came home from work to Angela in even more pain. Her doctor made one more suggestion and then called me to say that if this didn't work, it was time to go in. We followed her instructions. After a little while I suggested to Angela that we head into the Emergency Room. She said, "No, let's get some rest and hope I'll be better in the morning." At 2 a.m. she woke me up to say the pressure was too much to take. We loaded the kids in the car and headed to the hospital.

We fully expected that the ER docs would give her an enema, and she'd be ready to enjoy an Easter feast by that afternoon. Our children, Gianna and Augustine, waited with me in the waiting room while Angela was seen. As usual, it was a long wait and a long process. Around 6 a.m. I decided to take the kids down to the cafeteria for some food. As we got in line to order, Angela texted me that a nurse was trying to find me. I went back up to the waiting room with a little worry as I wondered what the nurse had to say. The nurse informed me that they did an X-ray; it showed an anomaly, and while they weren't too concerned, they were going to do a CT just to be sure. She said Angela could probably be out of here soon. With that my fear subsided, and I took the kids back down for some breakfast.

As we finished eating, Angela suggested that I take the kids home or out somewhere because it might be a little longer. Since we both thought this was no big deal, I took her advice and headed home. We got home and no sooner did we all sit on the couch then I got the next message, "The doctor wants to speak to us. You need to come back. I'm worried." I replied to her not to worry; they said it probably wasn't anything big.

As I put the kids in the car to head back to the hospital, I didn't immediately realize the severity. I had just assumed, as the nurse had already told me, the CT scan was routine and nothing to be worried about. But as I got on the road something clicked. The doctors didn't want to speak to Angela alone, but said her husband should be with her. Realizing that they wouldn't say this if it was "no big deal," my heart began to pound. I immediately asked Gianna if she would pray a Chaplet with me. We quickly recited the Divine Mercy Chaplet and rapidly spoke the words, "For the sake of His sorrowful passion, have mercy on us and on the whole world." With each decade my heart grew in anticipation of what would come. We sat in the car to finish. I knew by this point that I had to hand this over to God because I was about to walk into news of an unknown sort, the sort that we only see in movies and the sort that we play in our minds and hope and pray will never happen. The final three prayers of the Chaplet are prayed, "Holy God, Holy Mighty One, Holy Immortal One, have mercy on us and on the whole world." And as we recited one more prayer, I got the kids out of the car and took a deep breath. I felt that I was about to enter into a new world previously unknown to me. I was right.

I entered the emergency room and the receptionist immediately came over and asked, "Is there someone who can watch your kids?" I said I'd call someone, but it would take time and so they sent out a nurse to stay with them. The simple act of leaving my children in the waiting room with someone I did not know was a hard one. I had to resign in my head that my concern in this moment had to be for my wife, and I had to specifically offer this up to God. Truth be told, the fact that our son Augustine, who at the time didn't like going to strangers and even struggled going with people he knew, was completely unconcerned with my leaving the room was a small miracle in a list of many.

I came to my wife's side, and we quickly prayed. That's when the two doctors came in and gave the news. Oh the news that I wish I could erase! We talked about trusting and hoping. We talked about how we could get through this - we'd been through so much together. I asked Angela how she felt and she said, "I'm not surprised. I always somehow felt this sense that something like this would happen to me. I'm scared, but I'm not surprised."

After a few moments of talking and convincing each other that we would trust as we always have known to do, we asked permission to bring our children back to see Angela. Our friend Amy Jo was on her way to take them for the day, so we wanted to give them time with Angela and assure them that she would be okay. They thought we were still going to have Easter Sunday and didn't have a clue what was about to happen. I explained that Mommy was sicker than we thought and needed to stay at the hospital for a few days. It was near impossible for me to hold back the tears. Their sweet faces only reminded me of the situation we were facing. Their innocent, sweet, unknowing faces; how I wish I could take them back to that innocence, when they didn't know that storms would come in life and smash our hopes to pieces. We went back and they joyfully kissed their mom and showed her the stuffed animals the hospital had given them. Angela, with great poise, excitedly loved them and encouraged them, telling them they were going to have a fun Easter with Amy Jo. Once Amy Jo arrived, I put their car seats in her car and went back to my wife's side. As the day went on, we would learn little more except to know that the surgeons did not want to operate. We later learned surgery was not viable because her case was too severe.

I recall only a few details of the day but can vividly remember certain emotions. I remember making several trips that day to and from our house and the hospital to get things Angela needed and to take things to Amy Jo that she needed for the kids. On one of these trips, I remember walking into our house alone and feeling like I may not get to take Angela home ever again. It was one of the most gut-wrenching and empty feelings I have ever experienced. I wept and begged God to spare Angela's life. As the day went on I felt as if pieces of our life were crashing to the floor one by one. With each new realization of what might be, another "certainty" about our lives was shattered and my heart would break.

Late in the afternoon, I picked up Gianna and Augustine from Amy Jo's, and we took a short nap at home. Then I put them in the car and took them to have Easter with their mom. Earlier that day, I had picked up their Easter baskets and the gifts Angela had prepared for them and took them to her room so they could be surprised. It was two hours of pure joy for all of us. For me, it gave me hope to watch them interact with Angela and for her to give them her gifts. It helped me to see that perhaps the shattering that I experienced was only symbolic and that there was hope. For the kids, it was enough to save their memory of Easter Sunday.

TELLING THE NEWS

While Angela waited for a hospital bed that day, we decided together that we needed to let everyone know and ask for urgent prayers. We had called a few close people but felt very strongly that we needed lots and lots of prayers in this time. So that afternoon I posted the following message on my Facebook page:

Pray for Angela
Dear Friends,

This morning, as many of you were waking up and joining the Church in a great "Alleluia, Christ is Risen!" Angela and I received some sobering news. She has a large mass growing in her colon and also a possible tumor on her liver and her ovary. While doctors will not confirm without a biopsy, we have been told to prepare for cancer.

*We certainly hope for a miracle, but also know that it may
be a long road. We are prepared for either. I'm writing to ask
you all to pray, pray hard. One of the first things Angela said
to me this morning was, "Jesus still rose so, so don't worry."
Amen. I do believe. Please pray for us and for our long road
ahead. For today, they are letting her rest and hoping to
relieve some of the pressure through a tube that has been
inserted into her nose. In the morning they will try to get
a look at the mass and get a biopsy. At that point they will
decide on a course of action. Surgery is a definite, but the
question remains if it is cancer or not.*

*We most certainly believe in a God of miracles. We saw it
last year with our friend Melanie who should have died,
and we believe it is possible for Angela. We also know that it
is possible that God would allow us to go through this trial.
So, please pray for a miracle, but also pray for us to have the
strength we need for whatever God brings our way.
It is, of course, ironic that we would receive this news on
Easter Sunday. It is certainly sobering, but do not for a
moment allow it to steal your Easter joy. It has not stolen
ours.*

Thank you in advance for your prayers and your love.

*In Christ,
Chris Faddis*

With that simple note began an incredible outpouring of
support from our family, friends, and acquaintances from all over.
Word began to spread across social networks like wildfire, and

the prayer storm quickly picked up power. While it would still be a long and difficult few days, it was an incredible relief to have the power of so many prayers on our side. The day after her diagnosis, Angela wrote the following message on Facebook:

> ... for the thousands of prayers that are flying to heaven for my sake. There is no greater comfort than the Body of Christ all united for you. I am hopeful and in good spirits, spending the day in prayer and communion with my husband. Also, I'm physically feeling much better than I have been - I have a great team of nurses and doctors looking after me and helping me to be comfortable. I got my first sip of apple juice a few minutes ago and it was delicious! Tomorrow surgery is at 7 a.m. - first of the day!
>
> (Angela Faddis, April 25, 2011)

REALITY: THE LONG ROAD

The next day, after an exploratory procedure failed because the tumor was causing too much of a blockage, a team of surgeons came in, and without many words to cushion the blow, informed us that Angela had Stage IV colon cancer, and that most people would question surgeons being involved at all. The spread of the cancer was limited to the liver, but the liver was covered with multiple tumors. They told us their plan of action and after answering a few questions, they left the room. Their plan was that the following morning, they would go in and perform a liver biopsy to confirm the diagnosis; they would place a port in her chest to prepare her for chemotherapy, and then they would perform a diverting colostomy to allow her to pass stool. All of this was foreign and none of it made sense in that moment. The ring of those words "stage IV colon cancer" was deafening.

We were left with a sinking feeling in our guts as we allowed the news to set in that this was, in fact, life threatening. Each moment of this day was a painful realization of the situation we were in. As we cried together and prayed together, there was little solace except for the encouragement and love of friends, loved ones, and strangers far and wide whose words and prayers were like medicine for our aching souls.

We had a brief moment of reprieve when my co-workers and dear friends, DJ, Jen and BJ, came by to bring toys for the kids and encouragement for Angela and me. Their tears and their laughter brought such comfort to our day. Still, seeing the sadness on their faces was also a realization of what so many of our friends and loved ones were feeling. I recall a moment with the three of them outside of the room as they first arrived. As we talked and I recapped where things were, their eyes welled with tears and I saw the hurt they felt for us. We were not feeling this pain alone. It feels that way at first - as if you are alone, that no one else could actually feel what we were feeling. But in truth, we all have our place in each other's lives. Though not many could know what I as her husband was feeling or what Angela as the person in the hospital bed was feeling, they all felt it in their own way. DJ, Jen and BJ were in union with us in our suffering and they were going to see us through. They stood as a reminder of the many friends, family and strangers around the country who had already begun to band around us in prayer.

I spent much of the day trying to be strong for Angela but took many breaks to walk out of the room and breathe. These walks were so very difficult, partly because an unavoidable portion of the walk was going between buildings using a glass sky bridge which was sitting over the top of the morgue. As I would stand in that bridge and see a coroner's vehicle or a hearse, I would weep. I would continue my walk and just beg God that she not see that morgue anytime soon. These walks were also hard because I had to face the myriad of emotions, worries, fears, and "what ifs" that were before us. At least for the time, I had to face those questions alone. At one point, Angela was lucid enough to talk, and we had some sincere moments of crying for and with each other, sharing our feelings and encouraging one another to not give up hope. In one very difficult moment Angela said, "All this time that I've had depression I felt like I was dying inside. I just wanted to die. Now that I'm better and I feel alive, I actually am dying, or at least I could be." But in retrospect, that depression most certainly paved a path for Angela's faith. The many times when she had to choose to believe in God, in His love, in His purpose for her life, even when she could feel nothing but despair, were like a training ground. Still, it was hard for Angela and me to understand how we could come through that great trial of her depression only a couple months before and find ourselves facing an even greater trial. After some time talking and praying through that, we began making and returning the many phone calls to family and close friends. Angela, who does not like the phone, was exhausted after only a couple calls and went to sleep.

I went to be with the kids that night. Knowing that I'd have to be at the hospital early the next morning, we felt it was important that I spend the evening with them. So I could get up and leave them in bed in the morning, we decided for the kids and me to sleep at the Reynolds family's house. The Reynolds family were dear friends in Winston-Salem whose son was only a couple of weeks older than our son Augustine. Angela and Katie had gone through pregnancy together and become very close. I arrived at Angela's side early and sat with her while she woke up and waited for them to take her down to surgery. We prayed together and talked a little, and then I held her hand as they wheeled her down to the Operating Room. Letting her go was difficult. I knew that the surgery was fairly routine, but as the surgeon had said, it was three minor surgeries at once, which made it major. Also, knowing that Angela's cancer was advanced, I knew that there were a lot of potential complications. My only response at this point was to take it to the one place I knew I would be able to let my worry go. I went to Mass. I got there a little late, but as I walked in, I knew I was where I needed to be. I recall the prayers of the Consecration being particularly profound for me. I recall weeping quite a bit, but I also remember the feeling of a weight being lifted as I focused not on me, not on Angela, not on our children or on the myriad of worries or concerns we now had, but on God. One thing I have learned throughout this journey is why the Mass is such a significant form of worship; it seeks to draw us out of ourselves. It pulls our eyes, our hearts, our minds and our person outside of ourselves. Regardless of your practice of worship, I believe it is essential that our worship draw us out of ourselves to focus on God. I can't count the amount of times during the last couple of years when overwhelming feelings have been lifted just in reciting and singing the prayers of the Mass.

I left Mass that morning with a particular sense of hope. As I went to the hospital, I was happy to see two dear friends waiting in the surgical waiting room and praying. We prayed together, we talked, we laughed, and we hoped. The surgeon came out and gave me the rundown. Surgery had gone well, but he confirmed that there were significant masses on the liver. He also confirmed that while they needed the biopsy results, he was certain it was colon cancer. I had hoped that perhaps it was all benign, but he made it clear that we were in for the long haul. The realization that this was going to be a long journey began to set in for both of us. There was no simple quick fix. There was no surgery, no miracle treatment. Save a divine intervention, we were on a path that would not end anytime soon.

Angela, though keeping a positive attitude, was in a great deal of pain. At times the pain, combined with the fear and worry, were too much for her. She spent a lot of time crying those next couple of days. Piled on top of this was the fact that Angela was missing Gianna's 4th birthday. Our dear friends, the Reynolds, did a great job of making Gianna's day special. Angela encouraged me to leave for a few hours to spend the day with Gianna. I took her to the mall where we had promised she could do one of those bungee bounce attractions when she turned four. For a little while, we were in heaven. My coworkers and their families also surprised Gianna with an impromptu birthday party at her favorite restaurant, complete with presents, cake and an ice cream sundae. These little joys helped me, the kids, and even Angela to cope with the gravity of our new crisis.

THE STORM RAGES ON

It seems that most storms we go through in life are temporary. They last for a day, a week, a month or a little more. It was clear now that this storm would not go away anytime soon. We began then to reflect on our resolve to trust. We must trust, not in a quick fix or a momentary solution, but in a God who will see us through any trial. This became our focus. We decided we would live fully every day that we had, we would hope and pray for a miracle, and we resolved together to trust, no matter what.

Not one of us will go through life without passing through storms. Not one. Some of us may pass through some more difficult storms than others, but not one of us will go this road fully unscathed. Some storms will go away quickly. Others will not. These storms in life come in all forms. They come in job loss and the pain of divorce; they come in watching a family struggle with drug addiction; they come in the pits of depression and despair; they come in financial struggle, and they come in deceit of friendship. Storms can be in the form of infertility, loneliness, self-doubt, major car accidents, and in losing someone suddenly. They can be cancer, heart attacks, and death.

What then is our response? Do we cower? Do we settle into despair? Do we wail and cry? Jesus told us, "In the world you will have trouble, but take courage, I have come to conquer the world" (John 16:33). The disciples faced the greatest of storms and even though the Messiah was physically present on the boat, they cried out in fear: "Master, master save us, we are perishing" (Luke 8:24). Christ calms the storm, but He also says, "Where is your faith?" (Luke 8:25). Yes, sometimes in these storms we cry out. We are fearful. We worry, we doubt, we are scared, but all the while Christ stands at our side saying, "Be still and know that I am God…" (Psalm 46:10), whispering words of calm and consolation, promising that He has conquered the world, and reminding us that He has prepared a place for us.

Storms, they come and go, just as the good and beautiful things in our lives do. The honeymoon periods of life, the perfect relationships, jobs, houses, and vacations, they all come and go. None of this is permanent; all of it will pass. All of it will come to an end, save one thing: the promise of heaven and eternal salvation, the promise that Christ will go and prepare a place for us. These promises are the ultimate shelter from the storm. They are our ultimate hope and consolation. These storms, they are nothing. These trials, they are nothing. They all will pass.

It Is Well

WHY GOD, WHY?

Nestled in her hospital bed with a tube placed to relieve
pressure and plenty of medication to numb the pain, Angela
attempted to rest. For now at least, things were calm. The halls
of the hospital were quiet and there wasn't a whole lot going
on during this Easter Sunday. I took a walk. The quiet of those
halls was comforting but deafening. There was no safety for my
thoughts there. At each turn of the hall, I would be pierced again
with the sharpness of that word spoken only a short time ago:
cancer. Cancer? How? Why? Cancer? Really? Not Angela, not my
healthy Angela! Not the woman who avoided all the foods that
caused cancer and ate all the foods that prevented it. Not my active
and vibrant wife. I thought for a moment to pray. I thought for a
moment to take some time to play some church music and sing, to
take my mind past the pain. I thought...

How does one sing when the only sound that comes is a
shrill cry of utter terror at the thought of this crisis before you?
How does one sing when all that comes out is the cry, "Why God,
why?" When your wife lies in a bed riddled with a disease that

silently and secretly grew inside for years before suddenly making itself known. How do you sing? How do you pray?

I decided to take leave of this place for a little while. I kissed Angela and went home. I could be safe there - safe to think, to cry, to yell, and maybe to play some church songs and try to bring my mind past the pain for a moment.

I sat down, I opened my computer, and I searched for it. The song. The one song that had marked our journey of trust. The song I long reflected on and desired to write a book about. The song that Angela and I would often remind one another of. Many months and years had passed since the song, "It is Well with My Soul" struck a chord in my heart and made me look to find out the story behind its powerful words. Often we think of the great hymns of our Church and assume they were written in the solitude of an organ loft. But something about these words struck a chord, and I knew there must be a story behind the song. I went look-ing and I found Horatio Spafford, a successful business man in Chicago who had done well in life. But in 1871, his only son died at the age of four. Soon after, he lost a great deal of property in the Great Chicago Fire which took most of his wealth. These two blows would be enough to cripple many. Yet, Spafford carried on in faith. A couple years later, he had planned to vacation with his family in Europe. His family went ahead of him as he got held up by busi-ness. While at sea, the ship carrying his wife and children collided with a larger ship and sunk immediately. His four daughters all perished.

I found the song, turned it on and tried to sing. I couldn't sing. I couldn't get out the words. I thought: How? How can I sing? How can I say "it is well" when it most certainly is not. Our life is shattered to the ground in a million pieces. Glass shattered all over. At each moment I found another piece of glass, I heard another crash. I thought: "Will she see Gianna graduate? Will she see Augustine become a man? Will she be there to comfort Gianna in the way only a mother can?" Our life was shattered on the ground and with every attempt to sing, a pain hit my chest. But I couldn't pray; the silence was too deafening. The only way in this moment for me to turn to God was to sing.

Somehow I forced myself, I gritted my teeth, I fought past the tears and I sang that first "It is well" since those horrible words: "Cancer is all over and we're really late." "It is well." Horatio said it as he passed over the place that swallowed his daughters whole. He could have stood in that place and cursed the seas and the skies for causing that storm. He could have cursed the ship's captain for not steering a safer course; he could have cursed God himself. But instead, he blessed the God of all things. He blessed God who makes all things new, and he said those words that I could barely come up with the strength to say on this day when my life was shattered: "It is well." I sang those words through tears and heartache. Somehow those words gave me calm. They reminded me that no matter the cost, my life, our life is not our own. It all belongs to God. "Whatever my lot, thou hast taught me to say, it is well, it is well, it is well with my soul."

"Thou hast taught me to say." You see, we can sing, we can proclaim faith in the midst of trial because it is written. It is written not only in a book and on pages of centuries told. It is written on our hearts. It is written on my heart. It was written on Angela's heart. So when she should have been crying out, "Why, God, why?!" she said the only thing her heart knew to say. It was not some trite response that she memorized for this moment. It was not a cliche that she had to recite in Sunday school. Her heart, her heart knew one thing for certain: Jesus still rose. This was Easter Sunday and though it felt a hell of a lot like being crucified on Good Friday, her heart knew that the Resurrection was still real and was still the promise we had in Christ, so she said, "Jesus still rose, so we will trust." So I sang. How could I keep from singing? The song was written on my heart, on her heart long ago. If she, lying in a bed riddled with a disease that could likely take her life, could say the words, then I had no choice but to sing.

PASSING OVER THE STORM

Horatio had lost it all. It would be no surprise to anyone if he gave up at this point, if he threw his fist in the air and said some choice words to God. Yet, Spafford's response was the complete opposite. While on his way to meet his wife in Europe, he passed near the place where his daughters had died and was inspired to write these words: "When peace like a river, attendeth my way, when sorrows like sea billows roll; whatever my lot, thou hast taught me to say, it is well, it is well, with my soul."

That Horatio could even look to God again is a testament to the working of faith and grace in his life. He was literally passing over the greatest tragedy, the greatest storm in his life, and was able to say, "It is well with my soul." He did not respond in anger but in faithfulness. Do Spafford's words suggest that he had no grief, no sadness, no anguish? Certainly not. But in acknowledging all the pain, the tragedy, the hurt, he had the faith to proclaim that the promise of Christ remains the same, that God is good no matter the hardships in life. I imagine that this couple years of Horatio's life are not unlike the imagery of the storm in the last chapter. "The waves crashed the sides of the boat like the strike of a wrecking ball, tossing the boat this way and that... This storm will not give way, the passengers in tow wondered if they would see the light of another day." Yet, he chose to trust that God's promise was still true.

When I first researched the story behind this song, I was working on writing a book about trust. I did not know what the title would be, but the sentiment of this song resounded so much in my heart. I often would remark to Angela that I felt like it would be such a powerful witness if someone wrote a book on trust from the middle of the storm. If someone could write a book on trust while they were in the thick of it, still broken, still lost and confused, that would be such an incredible witness to the world. I would continually pick up my pen to write and then for some reason - be it discouragement, or personal trials, or the busyness of life - I'd declare I wasn't ready to write this book and stop. Once I learned the story of Horatio Spafford and his family, I was floored by the amount of faith and resolve it must have taken to pen these words. I know in myself how hard it is to sing words like these at Mass when I'm facing a difficult time. Somehow this man's faith pulled him from his grief and called him to proclaim that no matter the trials of this earthly life, it is well with his soul because he knows the promise of Christ, the promise of salvation. I never finished writing that book, but I knew that somewhere down the road, I would write this type of book and I knew the title would be taken from this profound song. This book was written on my heart and as Angela's and my lives intertwined, it became a passion of her heart as well. It was a frequent topic of conversation and a frequent topic of talks we would each give to teenagers and other groups.

SHE HAD A MUSTARD SEED...

When Angela became ill, it was no wonder that she would say the words, "Jesus still rose, so we will trust." Her heart, though often troubled, was firmly resolved to trust Christ no matter what. Angela and I had often wondered how hard it was for Spafford to pen the words of "It is Well" when passing over that horrific storm in his life. Literally passing through the pain and heartache of losing your children must have been excruciating, yet he chose to allow the words of this song to well up in his heart and be written down for all to hear and sing.

Angela too, in the scariest, most tragic moment of her life, allowed her faith to well up within her and chose to trust, to believe, and to hope. Her simple words, "Jesus still rose, so we will trust" came from deep within her soul, from the place where her faith had been built up and her trust had resided for many years. Being so close to her in that scary moment and the many moments that followed, I can say that those words were most certainly from her heart. Yes, she had moments of sadness, profound despair, and fear. Yet through each of those moments and periods on this journey, she would allow her faith to well up within her and like a spring of living water, her faith would give her new life each step of the way.

A year into Angela's journey, she found a quote from Pope Benedict XVI that she loved, and I think it illustrates so well the faith that allowed Angela to say, "Jesus still rose..." She posted it on her Facebook page on April 12, 2012: "I have a mustard seed and I'm not afraid to use it." These simple words became a motto for Angela, and she was overjoyed when she found them. She said it spoke of the desire of her heart. We had often discussed that it would be easy to give up hope, but because of our faith we simply could not. While she did not find these words until later on in her journey, they were most certainly true of her life. She always chose her faith in spite of any pain or hardship. Prior to her cancer diagnosis, Angela would choose to trust in Christ even when her depression was at its worst. She would say, "I don't feel God, I don't feel like He loves me, but I know that He does. So I can't give up hoping." Having been by her side in those moments, I can say that it took true courage to come to that place of trust in the midst of the pain she was in. Often in those moments, she would turn to me and say, "I need you to pray for me, to say the words for me." I would, and together we would cling to Christ and beg him to pull her out. Yes, she had a mustard seed, and she most certainly used it.

I would add to Pope Benedict's words that sometimes we have a mustard seed, and we have no clue how to use it. In those moments, Angela would still pull out that mustard seed and ask God to show her how to use it. I think that is the essence of Angela's story; she always allowed her faith to lead her.

Two months after her diagnosis she shared the following message on her Facebook support page:

By the Grace of God
Today was an emotional one. Coming to the end of our first round of chemo...listening to the doctor talk about my

symptoms, the amount of cancer in my body, and the goal of surgery to come...it is still shocking. It is often hard to hear people commenting on "my strength" or my "great faith." Being able to fully trust in God has been a desire of my heart for a long time, but a challenging one. I think that we have reached a point where we have just realized that we have no other choice. Living in despair is just not an option. We have children for whom our greatest desire is to teach them of God's love for us.

I have heard many great spiritual teachers in the past say that when you are healthy and doing well...that is when you need to build up your prayer life, storing up those prayers and that grace for when life's toughest moments come your way. I don't feel like I did enough of that...and yet, it has never been easier for me to trust in God than it is now. I truly believe that the hope I have is not for any greatness in me, but by the grace of God! This time of physical weakness has given me tender moments with my children in prayer and discussions of faith. It has also given me opportunities to read and pray for others struggling with similar challenges or things that I find to be even more heart-breaking. My love and compassion for others has been expanded. I don't downplay my pain. It is real and valid. And so is the pain of my brothers and sisters. I pray for a miracle for myself. I trust that God has even bigger plans for me. And I hope that my journey can bring hope and God's love to those following, not for any "strength" of my own, but through my honest openness to God's Awesomeness!

(Angela Faddis)

You see, it is enough for us to simply have faith, to have that mustard seed, and we can use it by the grace of God. We don't often know how to use it, but God does. Our only requirement is to call on that gift of faith, to allow it to well up in us and, as Angela says, to "build up" that faith and life of prayer when things are well.

Angela would often speak to teenagers about the need to build up their faith when things were good, to learn to pray even when everything was great. She would tell them that they need to build up their faith and seek Christ now before the world gets in the way. She would share about her own faith and how often it was hard for her to pray or to trust in God, but of how the faith life she had when she was young always carried her through. This was one piece of advice Angela wanted to leave for the world. In a radio interview she was asked what she would want to share with others that she has learned from all of this. She said, "For those of you who aren't in a period of suffering, take the time now to deepen your prayer life, because you just never know what's going to happen, and to know the love of Jesus before encountering something like this is something I am so grateful for, and I wish everyone could experience." When the cancer journey began and as it continued, there were so many times that Angela would say to me how grateful she was for her faith because at times it was impossible to pray. But she knew she could simply rely on the graces of all those days before. She would just say, "God, I can't pray right now, but I need your grace."

As our story went on, that mustard seed of Angela's faith and my faith, along with countless thousands is what carried us through. God proved to Angela and me that it was possible to "fully trust in God" as Angela mentioned above. Step by step, God allowed us to give over more and more of ourselves to Him and to allow Him to lead the way. It seems in a way that God allowed this trial so that He could prove to us not only that it was possible to trust Him completely, but also that He had given us the faith and grace we needed to do so. As stated above, Angela didn't think she did enough building up of her prayer life, and yet she felt like it was never easier to trust in God. Our loving Father sometimes allows trials and sufferings in our lives in order to prove to us that "[His] grace is sufficient" (2 Corinthians 12:9).

It is my sincere hope that in the pages of this book, you too will see that it is possible to trust God completely with your life. I hope you will see that in the high points of great happiness and in the pit of suffering, you can entrust your life to God. When you can have in yourself this disposition of trust in God no matter what, then you can say "it is well" in the midst of any storm, any trial, any sorrow in your life. I pray that you would find that you have that same mustard seed of faith, and though it may seem small and insignificant to you, that little mustard seed is enough to not only move mountains, but also to move your heart to complete and utter dependence on God.

Yes, you and I will both continue to have trouble in our lives. We will continue to find ourselves in those "Why, God?" moments of life, but with prayer and constant turning ourselves back to God and trusting Him with our lives, we can find a faith welling up within us that brings us great peace, comfort and joy. Indeed, friends, it is well because God has not forgotten us. His promise remains. May you find in the pages of this book a witness to the hope we find in the gospel, and may you too, allow your faith to well up within your soul to sing a beautiful song of praise to our loving God and Father in heaven.

Shelter

"For you have been a stronghold to the poor, a stronghold to the needy in his distress, a shelter from the storm and a shade from the heat."

(Isaiah 25:4)

It was the Monday after Easter; Angela and I had learned that day of the severity of her disease. I was driving to the Reynolds' family home where my children were staying. I was listening to the new album by a Christian group called, Jars of Clay. The title song, "Shelter" was playing as I pulled in front of their home. Standing in the window of their storm door was my daughter, Gianna, and behind her was the Reynolds family with my son, Augustine, standing at their feet. At that moment I was struck with gratitude as I heard the line, "May this place of rest in the fold of your journey bind you to hope, you will never walk alone." The song continues into the chorus, "In the shelter of each other, we will live, we will live."

This moment was an overwhelming moment for me. As I looked and saw my children being cared for in the shelter of a loving family, I felt and heard all of the countless prayers that were being cried out to heaven for my wife and our family. I sat in that moment for a minute while I cried tears of gratitude. I knew then, and I continued to be reminded, that we were being loved and cared for physically and spiritually as countless people stepped forward and, as one friend said, "stood in the gap" for us.

THE CALL TO REMAIN FAITHFUL

As the storms of life rage on, the torrential rain comes down and the powerful winds blow with great force knocking us this way and that, and we can find great hope in the words of Isaiah: "For you have been a stronghold to the poor, a stronghold to the needy in his distress, a shelter from the storm and a shade from the heat" (Isaiah 25:4). We have witnessed His stronghold as He held fast though we cowered and shuddered in the face of each new trial. As we allowed ourselves to turn to Him, to cling to Him, God remained steadfast and strong in every way - even while our knees would buckle. Even when we would shout to Him in lamentations, even when we would pout and throw a tantrum, God was a stronghold and remained steadfast for us.

There goes the saying "sometimes God calms the storm - sometimes He calms his child." We often assume that by prayer we are going to get the storm to lift, and sometimes it will. But often we find that a storm comes and it stays. We call this long suffering- the kind of suffering that lasts and the kind of trial that must be trudged through over a long period. Yes, while God does answer prayer and does lift the clouds of the storm in many ways in our lives, He will often allow the storm to continue.

In these times it is easy to wonder why God isn't answering our prayer or taking away the pain and trial. Yet in these times, even if He allows the downpour to continue, He is still faithful. He promises us trouble, but He also promises us that He conquered it all (cf. Jn 16:33). He promises that He will be with us through it all, comforting us, consoling us, guiding us and sheltering us from the storm (cf. Mt. 28:20).

As Angela and I began to realize that this journey would not be a quick and easy one, that our miracle may not come anytime soon and it may not come at all, we had to come to terms with that feeling of dread - of what might lie ahead. Yet we also in some way felt this sense that God would use our journey for His glory in our lives and possibly the lives of others. We certainly hoped the way He would use it would be in a monumental miracle that would be so magnificent that people would have no doubt it was God's hand, however we knew that God might be calling us to be faithful on a long road of suffering. So we prayed for His grace, strength and provision. The great thing about God is that though He does allow suffering to befall us, He also is ever faithful.

Immediately after I posted the news of Angela's diagnosis, an outpouring of love and support began, first from our family and friends and then from many people from around the country who had heard our story from their family and friends. The emails, Facebook notes and phone calls were a sure sign that the people of God had our back in prayer. A few days later, our friend Melanie Pritchard put up a Facebook page to help direct people to a place to leave us messages and offer support. That page grew quickly and those messages of love continued to pour in. While Angela was in the hospital, people from our parish in Winston-Salem began coordinating meals, help with cleaning the house and some even helped me completely redecorate, rearrange and clean the house for Angela. Melanie had also set up a donation link and donations began to pour in. I hadn't yet realized the financial need we would have, but it was nice to know the money was there if we needed it. Even as I prayed for God's help with all of these temporal and material needs, He provided in ways I could not have ever fathomed. His provision comes to us through the hands of those around us and those who step forward to stand in the gap. As the Jars of Clay song says, "In the shelter of each other we will live." We often wonder when and how God will provide for us in times of need. He most certainly acts through the goodness of others as we so clearly learned.

In addition to the material and temporal help that was offered by so many, the incredible amount of prayer was like a balm of healing for our broken hearts. As I shared in a previous chapter, Angela shared these words regarding these countless prayers: "For the thousands of prayers that are flying to heaven for my sake, there is no greater comfort than the Body of Christ all united for you." As the week went on, we would hear from people from all over the world: convents in other countries offering prayers and sacrifices for us, whole youth groups, churches and the like gathering in prayer. Several friends were in Rome that week for the Beatification of my hero and spiritual father, Blessed John Paul II. I'll never forget the message shared with me from a long-time friend, Randy Raus saying, "We just finished praying at the tomb of John Paul II for Angela Faddis." I rushed into Angela's room to tell her, and we both smiled with a sense of relief. It's as if knowing that the Body of Christ was surrounding us in prayer was all we needed to be okay.

One of the more profound examples of this shelter and
God's providence came a little over two months after Angela's
diagnosis. She had finished two rounds of chemotherapy and we
had new CT scans and blood work done. Things had been looking
up and doctors were hopeful we were making progress. The day
of our follow up appointment happened to be our fifth wedding
anniversary, July 1, 2011. The long and the short of it is that the
visit revealed the chemotherapy was not working. Thankfully, we
had scheduled a vacation to go back to Phoenix to see family and
friends just two days later. It was a much needed break. We arrived
in Phoenix and saw several friends after we got off the plane. It
was a joyful and tear-filled reunion. During this little gathering,
Melanie Pritchard let us know she had made some calls and set up
some appointments with local doctors to discuss other options for
treatment. Melanie and I had talked several times about moving
Angela back to Phoenix. It was certainly what Angela and I wanted
to do, but we didn't see how it would be possible. We decided to
take these appointments anyway and see what was available. After
a couple of appointments, we were convinced that this was the
route we would like to go. The question of how we would do this
remained. I had a job in Winston-Salem, we had a new lease we
had just signed on a bigger home and lots of other reasons to stay
put, yet we just knew this was the best thing for Angela, not just on
account of the treatments; her heart was home in Arizona.

So we prayed and decided we would trust God to figure out
the rest. A big part was figuring out how to pay for advanced treatments not covered by insurance. The expected total was going to be
around $120,000. The clinic was able to shave off quite a bit of that
cost, but there was still a lot of money to come up with, plus the

cost of moving, looking for a new job and finding a place to live. We went back to Winston-Salem after our nine day vacation and simply trusted God would show us how to get back. As we were walking onto the plane, I got a text message: "Found you a place to live for free." I responded to our friend to find out that another friend who was getting married in a few months had decided to move home with her parents until her wedding and was giving us her home for about three and a half months rent and utility free! As we walked the jet way to the plane, Angela and I had tears streaming down our face. God was literally providing a shelter for our family.

Angela had a surgical procedure scheduled for the day after we returned. That afternoon I set up an online fundraising page and simply asked people to help me save Angela's life. I told Angela that if we could raise $10,000 by the end of the week, I would feel much better about moving, however we planned to leave for Phoenix that next weekend either way. By the second night of the fundraiser we had already raised $10,000, and by the end of the week, we had raised $18,000. In total that fundraiser raised over $35,000 in 45 days and other fundraisers raised the rest, including a dinner event my family and some friends at Our Lady of Mount Carmel parish put on that raised $13,000.

The morning I received the news that we had reached our initial goal of $30,000, which was the minimum needed for treatment, I wrote the following post:

An Unbelievable Journey | Thank You!
As I woke up this morning, my phone buzzed which alerted me to a new email, an email that would tell me that a gen-

erous donor had taken us over our initial goal. A little while later, Angela and I put the kids in the car and headed out to take her to the treatment center.

As I sit and enjoy my coffee at home, I can't help but be overwhelmed. On July 1st, we found out that our course of treatment wasn't effective and we headed back to Phoenix for a week of rest. Here we are, on August 13, living in Phoenix and getting a whole new course of treatment - thanks to you.

It is hard to put into words the whirlwind that this last month and a half has been. We were in Phoenix for a week, went back to Winston where Angela would have another procedure, and then five days later, we packed our car and drove 2100 miles across the country. After settling here, I went back, packed up the rest of our things, loaded a Penske truck and drove another 2100 miles across the country. Now we are home and Angela is 1/3 of the way through her new treatment protocols.

On top of that, we went out on a limb when we made this decision, trusting that God would provide through the generosity and faithfulness of others, and here we sit having reached our initial goal, which was the minimum we would need to undergo this course of treatment. 339 people helped us reach that goal online and there are countless more who have helped with other donations and means of support. Amazing.

We know without a shadow of a doubt that this move was the right move, and we are confident that God is working in all of this. Angela's treatment schedule is vigorous and exhausting, but with each round, we know that she is getting better. Prayer is effective and it is an amazing feeling to know that we are wrapped not only in the loving arms of God, but in the loving arms of the hundreds and thousands of prayer warriors and supporters at our side.

As Gianna, Augustine, and I sat down for breakfast after dropping Angela off, Gianna asked me about who I loved. She wanted to know if I loved our friends as much as I love her and Augustine and Angela. I explained that I love them first and that our love is different. Then she said, "Well I love everyone, all of our friends - even the ones I don't know - you know all the people who are praying for us. I love them, too." Please know that you are making a difference for this little family, and even our children can see and feel it. The reality is that we still hope to raise the rest of our goal, but we continue to realize that it is not up to us to worry about that. God has provided the funds through those who are called to give, and he has provided for our needs and continued to provide work for me. So we will continue in hope that all of our needs will be met through work and through the continued generosity of others.

With all our love and gratitude,
Chris, Angela, Gianna, and Augustine

The ways in which God provided through His people are countless. I've had people ask me, "Why doesn't the Church just take care of your family. You're obviously very involved; couldn't they just take care of this?" My answer: the Church is taking care of us. The Church being the people of God who are praying, giving and assisting in countless ways. That is what God calls us to, to take care of one another in prayer, in aid, and sometimes through financial help. God's grace is powerful in that it does not seek to work on its own, but it seeks to work in and through us. Each of us. God desires us to participate in His works of grace. That happened in profound ways as people we had known for years and people we had never met and may never meet stepped forward in prayer and in help.

The ways in which the people of God - the Church - responded to our need in prayer and temporal support was an incredible vision of the Communion of the Saints in action. Simply put, the Communion of the Saints refers not solely to the saints in heaven. It refers to the people of God at all stages of their pilgrimage to heaven. That would include those of us on earth who are making our way to heaven (pilgrims), those in purgatory who are going through a time of purification, and of course those who are fully perfected and in heaven. In short, it is the family of God at all stages of their journey. As people all around prayed for us, sought the prayers of the saints in heaven, offered their own sufferings for our sake and the like, they were witnesses to what God desires for His family. A supporter wrote this to Angela on our "Save a Life" campaign page:

> "...and remember always to welcome strangers, for by doing this, some people have entertained angels without knowing it" (Hebrews 13:2). Angel is definitely part of your name. We do not know you or your family. In fact, we probably live hundreds of miles apart. A Facebook posting told us of your

story and God reminded me of the verse. You are in our
prayers. He is blessing you and your family."

It was a great reminder at the time of how God is working through this all. Not just blessing our family, but also blessing those who are praying for us and supporting us, bringing us all together through this trial.

One of the greatest blessings Angela received during this alternative and advanced treatment was a huge relief in side effects and the like. She had been experiencing so many side effects from the aggressive chemotherapy. The new treatments were working on building up her body as well as fighting the cancer. She wrote this update about a third of the way into her new treatment: "This is how you are helping me...Thank you! Thank you! Every prayer and every dollar is not only putting me on the path to full recovery, but it has improved my quality of life."

Shelter from the storm. Shade from the heat. Stronghold in our time of distress. Despite the long burden, the long-suffering, the pain and the heartache, we were not alone. In the "shelter of each other," God gave us new life each day and His mercy and grace were carrying us through. As the journey continued, we would continue to be reminded of this. God provided for every single need. Days would come in which Angela or I could not pray, but we knew that so many were praying for us, and in this we found incredible comfort. We would come up against a very big hurdle, either in her treatment or financially, and out of nowhere, God would provide the answer.

Jesus tells us clearly in the Gospel of Matthew that we ought not worry about our life. He tells us clearly that God will provide for our needs, yet how often do we live believing that to be true? I believe that the greatest lesson God gave to Angela, our children and me through this journey was that He would provide. I close this chapter encouraging you to reflect on Jesus' words in the Gospel, for our story is most certainly evidence of its profound truth.

Therefore I tell you, do not worry about your life, what you will eat [or drink], or about your body, what you will wear. Is not life more than food and the body more than clothing? Look at the birds in the sky; they do not sow or reap, they gather nothing into barns, yet your heavenly Father feeds them. Are not you more important than they? Can any of you by worrying add a single moment to your life-span?

Why are you anxious about clothes? Learn from the way the wild flowers grow. They do not work or spin. But I tell you that not even Solomon in all his splendor was clothed like one of them. If God so clothes the grass of the field, which grows today and is thrown into the oven tomorrow, will He not much more provide for you, O you of little faith? So do not worry and say, 'What are we to eat?' or 'What are we to drink?' or 'What are we to wear?' All these things the pagans seek. Your heavenly Father knows that you need them all. But seek first the kingdom [of God] and His righteousness, and all these things will be given you besides. Do not worry about tomorrow; tomorrow will take care of itself. Sufficient for a day is its own evil.

(Matthew 6: 25-34)

Even if . . .

"Life is a furnace and the faithful live by the Shadrach-prayer of only 4 words: 'Even if he doesn't.' This world doesn't have anything that can burn down the faith of a heart on fire for God."

(Ann Voskamp)

HOPE BEYOND HOPE

The words of Ann Voskamp ring so true to me and testify so clearly to the kind of hope Angela claimed. The story of Shadrach, Meshach, and Abednego tells how King Nebuchadnezzar set up a golden statue, and it was decreed that the people of all nations and languages were to bow down before this golden statue whenever they heard the musical instruments sound. The king was informed that these three men whom he had appointed as administrators of the province of Babylon were not obeying this decree. The king became angry and sent for them at once. The story of what happens next helps illustrate Voskamp's poignant words:

King Nebuchadnezzar questioned them: "Is it true, Shadrach, Meshach, and Abednego, that you will not serve my god, or worship the golden statue that I set up? Now, if you are ready to fall down and worship the statue I made, whenever you hear the sound of the horn, pipe, zither, dulcimer, harp, double-flute, and all the other musical instruments, then all will be well - if not, you shall be instantly cast into the white-hot furnace; and who is the God who can deliver you out of my hands?" If our God, whom we serve, can save us - from the white-hot furnace and from your hands, O king, may he save us! But [even if he doesn't], you should know, O king, that we will not serve your god or worship the golden statue which you set up."

(Daniel 3: 14-18)

The king, of course, was infuriated and not only had them thrown in the furnace, but he also had it heated to seven times more than usual. It was so hot that the men who threw them in were burned up. However, Shadrach, Meshach and Abednego walked around the furnace and sang praises to God. The fire continued to be stoked and became hotter and hotter, yet the king saw that they were walking around. Not only that, a fourth person was seen walking around – an Angel of God. The king called the three men out, and his heart was converted at seeing the great power of God.

No, not even the hottest fires of this world can burn down the faith of a heart on fire for God. Faith in God means we live with hope. It means often times hoping even when it seems futile. It means believing that God can deliver us, and often times, He will. But it also means that at times, He may not, and if He does not deliver us in the way we desire, it means we still have faith and trust that His plan is perfect and He will make good of it all.

It seemed that perhaps things were getting better and it became easy to think that perhaps God was going to deliver Angela from this cancer and that her faith would save her from the furnace. Soon though, our faith and our hope would be challenged and we would have to decide if we truly would trust God, "even if…"

THINGS BEGIN TO CHANGE

It was now October. Angela had been undergoing advanced radiation treatments and very advanced and alternative therapies since July. The time had come to assess how her tumors were responding to the course of treatment. We knew that she was feeling better, had her energy back, was able to eat again, and overall her blood work had shown consistent signs of improvement. Previous scans showed some signs of improvement also, but it was time for a more detailed look.

Our hopes were high. Our expectations were that we would have some really good news to share. Instead we had more mixed results. We posted the following Facebook update on October 25, 2011:

> *Angela's PET scan did not give the news we had hoped for. On the positive side, the liver tumors are dying and the radiation will continue to work for several months. On the bad side, the treatment showed little to no effect on the colon and there are two new (small) tumors in the abdomen. So next we look at what options we have and meet with more specialists. The news is sobering for sure, but we will*

continue forward in hope. Angela said again, "All I can say is Jesus, we trust in You."

Those who have been through a cancer diagnosis know that this kind of news is par for the course. It can become hard to think of forward movement. To hope any longer at times seems futile. We made a long distance friend named Laurie through this journey whose husband was also battling late stage colon cancer. At one point she shared, "We would give up hoping and we've tried that, but we simply cannot." Angela and I shared this sentiment whole-heartedly. While we were often tempted to give up hoping, we simply could not.

Just as hope seemed lost, Angela again spoke clearly, "All I can say is Jesus, I trust in You." For even if God did not deliver her from this cancer, she was going to be believe, to hope and to trust that no matter what, God had her best in mind. For us, this hope meant believing that God was allowing this journey for a purpose. We knew that purpose was for one of two things. The first was that He would miraculously heal Angela and it would be such evidence of His goodness that it would convert many hearts and strengthen the faith of many more. The other possibility was that God would use this to make an example of what it means to trust even when all did not seem so well.

A DOWNHILL SLOPE

As we got the news that the advanced and alternative treatments did not prove miraculous, we were disheartened, but we were not in despair. This news in many ways was a lesson and a reminder to us to put our hope in God alone.

After this CT scan, we took some time to discern the next steps. We were referred to a new oncologist, but we also began looking into getting Angela in to Cancer Treatment Centers of America. Angela was instantly certain this was the place for her. They cared for their patients in the way Angela wanted to be cared for; they offered many complimentary treatments to help in quality of life and had a very good nutrition program – including some incredible food that we looked forward to eating every time we went. We also had to move a few days later, so we focused on moving our family. After we moved in and got settled, I began making the calls to get Angela into CTCA and worked on figuring out all of the many things that needed to be figured out. Angela began to get ill after moving and her energy, her appetite, and her pain all began to be a problem. On November 11, she was not doing well. She had a very high fever. After consulting with her physicians, we decided to take her in. She was admitted with suspicion of a very serious infection. This hospital stay was scary for many reasons. She was in the hospital for about nine days. The doctors never did figure out what the infection was, but she seemed to be doing better and they sent her home. We immediately began scheduling visits with her new oncologist. As we prepared for that, Angela became sick again. A couple days before Thanksgiving, I drove Angela back to the hospital and she was admitted once again. Her fevers were back, her pain was severe and she was experiencing a lot of other symptoms. This stay would take us into December.

Spending Thanksgiving at the hospital was very hard for Angela. She had already missed out on Easter Sunday and she loved this holiday and was just so sad to miss it. We did our best to make it special, bringing her a meal and sharing Thanksgiving dinner in her room. She insisted that I take the kids to my family's to celebrate the day and not confine them to a hospital. It was a scary time.

Both of these stays made us very aware of the danger Angela's life was in. The kids figured that out as well. One night, as I was laying the kids down to sleep, Gianna turned to me and said, "Dad, is Mommy..." She stopped, with a crackle in her voice. I encouraged her to continue, "I don't want to say it," she continued. I let her know she could ask me anything and after some soothing, she said with a cry, "Is Mommy going to die?" Oh the heartache. We cried together and I just held her tight as she wept. As she calmed I said, "Gianna, we are all going to die someday. Mommy is very sick and she could die from this cancer, but she is doing everything she possibly can to get better and we just have to pray very hard that she can get better." We talked some more and she asked a couple of questions and fell asleep.

I was up late that night, thinking, praying and reflecting on our life and what could come. That night I wrote Angela a letter:

Before you go...

I have no plans of saying goodbye to you anytime soon, and I hope that one day we look on this letter and laugh a little about it. But still, I've thought a lot about what the kids and I need before you go. If it is sooner than we hope, I just want a few things to help the kids and me down the road.

First, please know that you are a wonderful mother and wife. Your presence and your deep love are evident in every day. If you were gone tomorrow, I would be able to tell our children that you loved them well and you loved them with all that you are. And I too would know this in my heart. Being loved by you is an incredible gift.

There are some things that I would like if you go - things that I want to be able to have to remember you by and things I want to be able to share with the kids throughout life.

Your creativity is an incredible gift that I don't think you even realize. When you made felt food for the kids, it was an incredible gift. I was so happy that my wife had the ability to do such an amazing thing. I would like to have more of your creativity to remember you by. So I want to encourage and support you in making some things for the kids so they can always remember how their mom made them beautiful things. Whether it's felt food or a blanket - it's up to you.

Your care in dressing our children and trying to get good memories on camera is a beautiful thing. I love seeing how you dress them and how much joy you get out of making them look as precious as they are. I also love that you want pictures of good moments. I know I joke with you about the camera because we have the phones, but I also appreciate your desire to capture good moments. I want to encourage and support you in capturing our good moments. I want to ask that you capture our family as you see it. I want to remember how you see us. When the kids and I miss you, we will be able to look and see how you see us, and I'll be able to tell them how much you loved moments with them.

I know writing is not your favorite thing, and I can't even begin to think of what it would be like to write a letter to the kids for a time when you might not be around. I would never ask for that. But I would love if you would write each of them a letter of love. As far as we know, you will be around when they turn 18, so write it as if you are still here. But in case you go home early, would you write them for me? It can be one letter - it can be many - whatever you feel you can do...

I wrote this letter and prayed about whether or not to give it to her. In the end, I never did give her this letter. We did have a deep heart-to-heart about it, in which I shared the sentiments above. We talked about that conversation I had with Gianna, and Angela set her sights on living with great intention. While she was not able to do everything I asked for above, she most certainly took it to heart, evidenced in the passion and intent with which she loved our family in those coming days and months.

Angela was eventually released from the hospital in early December, but not without some severe side effects to the chemotherapy medications that were given to her. In addition to this, her chronic pain had increased as her liver had now swollen to over double its size. The major side effect of these two hospital stays was weight loss. In total she lost around 25 lbs. This was not good at all. A cancer patient's weight is a constant concern and any major weight loss can be a sign for alarm. Angela's fatigue worsened, her side effects and pain continued, but we focused on living. With Christmas coming up, we knew we had to really focus on making it special. Angela used every ounce of energy she had to make sure that Advent and Christmas were memorable and that the kids had the best Christmas. She never said it, but I'm pretty sure Angela had some of those same thoughts in the hospital that Gianna was having, and she planned that Christmas as if it was her last.

The week of Christmas we had Angela's first evaluation at Cancer Treatment Centers. During the course of our evaluation, it became obvious to us that surgical options were not being discussed at all. Previous to this, surgery always seemed an option. We questioned her primary oncologist about why they weren't considering surgery, and he made it clear he did not see any options. After four days of evaluation and meeting with doctors, we were able to see a surgical oncologist to discuss any possibilities for surgery and also to be able to ask a surgeon firsthand why surgery was not an option for Angela. This visit was very eye opening and also very sobering. We learned a lot more about Angela's condition and got a much better understanding of her prognosis. It wasn't information we wanted to hear, but we also wanted to know the truth. After this visit, we shared the following update with our Facebook supporters:

The Truth Hurts

We had of course hoped and prayed that perhaps this surgeon would see some possibilities, but in the end, what we got today was cold, hard reality. While it was hard to swallow, we appreciated his honesty and his candor. The bottom line is that medically speaking, Angela's cancer is incurable and most doctors do not see a whole lot of hope for Angela.

Essentially what he told us was that every surgical option available would most likely prove lethal for Angela.

Up to this point, nearly every doc we've spoken to has spoken in more hopeful terms and offered this carrot of hope that if we do "x" and it shrinks the tumors, we can hopefully do surgery. Unfortunately, as this surgeon shared - "that is a very big 'IF.'"

So, what does this mean?
Well as one other doctor put it, we can do chemotherapy, or we can begin looking at hospice and end of life care. This is a grim reality. They will not give a prognosis, but standard medical care with chemotherapy is said to provide a 2-5 year life extension for someone with advanced stage cancer.

Sobering News
This news is obviously not that new to us. We knew Angela's cancer was not considered curable, but we also still hoped that perhaps there was some Hail Mary pass out there for us. Medically speaking, there just isn't. So while our prayer for Angela's healing never ceases and our search for alternative means of treatment that will extend her life and possibly cure her does not end, we have accepted that it is quite possible that Angela will no longer be with us in the next few years.

We are sober, but not hopeless. For Angela, there is a mixture of sadness along with resolve to not waste any time with our children. Acceptance of this possible fate is not easy, but she is doing so gracefully.

True Hope
In all of this, we know that our true hope lies in God. It is easy to find hope in a certain treatment, or surgery or can-

cer center. It is easy to place our hope in a clinical trial or some other means, but in the end our hope is in Christ. Our faith urges us to seek healing and to never stop hoping. Our faith in Christ prompts us to pray for a miracle but also be willing to accept whatever outcome we are given. I am ready to accept God's will, but I am also in constant prayer that God would, in His loving mercy, heal Angela and give our kids and me a long life with her.

Still, our hope ultimately rests in heaven. As Angela posted a few days ago, this journey we are all on is about a journey to heaven. Unity with God in the Trinity is our ultimate vocation and to that end, we know that no matter the outcome, God's will be done.

"So let us confidently approach the throne of grace to receive mercy and to find grace for timely help" (Hebrews 4:16).

With this I ask you to continue your prayer for our family and if you see fit, beg God for a miracle on our behalf. Your intense prayer for us has been an incredible gift. How can we lose hope when we know that so many are seeking God on our behalf?

In addition to praying for Angela's healing, please also pray for wisdom and discernment for us as we do our best to live life in the midst of this trial.

Life goes on.
With love and gratitude,
Chris Faddis

A few days later Angela would share about her side effects, symptoms and course of treatment, and the hard reality with which we were faced. She wrote, "We are obviously facing a very serious and difficult reality, but we are hopeful and never give up our prayers for a miracle..."

The decision to trust God wasn't an issue for us, but there's something that happens when we choose to trust God; He takes us deeper and deeper into that trust. Will you trust Me now? Will you trust Me if this happens? At each point on this road, when Angela would get sicker or we'd find out a certain treatment hadn't work or we'd find out more about the severity of Angela's disease, it was as if God was asking us yet again, "Do you trust Me?"

Giving up hope was not a big temptation for us. It was assigning our hope to something other than God that became the biggest temptation. I think many of us do this every day. We take our belief in God's goodness and assign it to material or temporal things. In our case, we were assigning our belief that God could heal Angela to a certain treatment or course of therapy; God would use the chemotherapy to heal her, or the natural therapies or the advanced radiation. At each step, as we would get news that was disappointing, we would often find ourselves saddened that God didn't use this method or that to heal Angela. Yet in the end our hope was never in a certain treatment or treatment center or the like. Our hope lies solely in God and his promises. Often I think we were hoping for a medical miracle when the reality is that God could choose to heal Angela in any way he wanted. Angela referenced this in her update where she shared what she loved about CTCA and the model of care: "So what is so great about CTCA? ... The bottom line is they give me hope. I already have hope in the one thing that really matters, Jesus and the promise of the Cross, but CTCA is taking care of my physical needs in a way that honors my beliefs about the human body."

With each step, our reliance on God and our resolve that He was our only hope only grew. Angela's favorite scripture has always been Romans 8:28: "We know that all things work for good for those who love God, who are called according to His purpose." This scripture was imbedded into Angela's very nature, and as we faced the reality that death was likely imminent, it seemed she had a new resolve to trust in God because she knew He would work for her good.

We now had to live in an interesting dichotomy. On the one hand, we had to face the reality of Angela's death being likely. God does not call us to ignore reality. Faith does not mean that we ignore whatever we don't want to happen because we know God couldn't possibly let us go through that. Faith and hope require the exact opposite. They are always aware of the facts of life, of the realities at hand and the situations we face. With that in mind we had to face the fact that Angela's illness was terminal. But our faith also called us to something else: to trust and hope that God would heal Angela if He saw fit.

Even if He doesn't heal Angela, even if she never is whole again, will we trust God? Will we truly trust in Him? Shadrach said it plainly: surely our God can deliver us, but even if He doesn't, we will not turn away from Him. Taking a look back at his words, I think we can see a reflection of Angela's sentiments of faith. "If our God, whom we serve, can save us - from the white-hot furnace and from your hands, O king, may he save us! But [even if he doesn't], you should know, O king, that we will not serve your god or worship the golden statue which you set up." You see, Shadrach was aware that the reality was they were going to die in that furnace unless God would save them. Yet his faith was not in God saving him from the furnace; his faith was simply in God and His promise. For Angela the statement might look something like this:

If our God, whom I serve can save me from this deadly cancer may He save me! But even if He doesn't heal me, I know He will heal me in heaven. You should know that all things work for good for those who love God, who are called according to His purpose. I will place my trust in Him.

Surely we believe in miracles, and we believed it was possible for Angela to be healed. We believed with every part of our being that Jesus was still concerned with healing - physical and spiritual. But even if He didn't heal her, would we still believe? Would we turn away? King Nebuchadnezzar says it this way, "If you bow to these other Gods, all will be well." We were certainly tempted to turn away from God in our hope, to turn our hope to other goods or to simply say, "If God does not heal her we will not believe." But surely we could not give up our faith. The question comes: will you still believe, will you still have faith, will you still trust even if God does not raise His hands to help you, to heal you? It is very easy to blame God, to turn away from God and to see God as unloving and uncompassionate during these trials. Yet the faithful are called to something greater: to have hope beyond hope, to have trust even when it seems there is nothing to trust in. We are called by God to trust Him even more. It would have been easy for Angela and I to say, "You know what, God? We trusted You and You still let this horrible thing happen. We are done with You!" But what good would that have done?

We chose instead to trust Him, "even if He [didn't]" heal Angela. We chose to trust Him even if a thousand more painful trials fell upon our family. Why? Because as I said in an earlier chapter, our hearts were formed in faith and that faith would not allow us to give up hope. Over the course of our lives God has shown us His faithfulness in so many ways that we simply could not give up hope even if we tried.

Romans 8:28 was written on our hearts. Angela and I believed that no matter what, that even if God didn't heal Angela, He would not leave our side; His promise of heaven remained and in the end, that promise of heaven was what Angela truly desired. Romans 8 continues:

What will separate us from the love of Christ? Will anguish, or distress, or persecution, or famine, or nakedness, or peril, or the sword? No, in all these things we conquer overwhelmingly through Him who loved us. For I am convinced that neither death, nor life, nor angels, nor principalities, nor present things, nor future things, nor powers, nor height, nor depth, nor any other creature will be able to separate us from the love of God in Christ Jesus our Lord.

This is why I can echo Ann Voskamp's words with great confidence: "This world doesn't have anything that can burn down the faith of a heart on fire for God."

The Clockman and the Things That Last

"'How much would you pay for an extra day,'" she said through a crackling voice. I began to listen from the other room as I thought she might be crying. She collected herself and began again, "'How much would you pay for an extra day?' The clock man asked the child. 'Not one penny,' the answer came…" Her voice began to break again. "Gianna, I just can't read this right now," I heard. Gianna protested, "Why can't you? I like this one!" "I just can't, Honey, please ask Daddy to read it." I went to them and took the book from Angela's hand. As I began to read, I slowly realized why Angela could not finish this poem.

"The Clock Man" by Shel Silverstein

"How much will you pay for an extra day?"
The clock man asked the child.
"Not one penny," the answer came,
"For my days are as many as smiles."

"How much will you pay for an extra day?"
He asked when the child was grown.

"Maybe a dollar or maybe less,
For I've plenty of days of my own."

As I neared the last verse, I too began to choke up.

"How much will you pay for an extra day?"
He asked when the time came to die.
"All of the pearls in all of the seas,
And all of the stars in the sky."

I understood why Angela couldn't finish. She had read this poem once before, and it hadn't hit her till the end, but this time, she knew what was coming. I believe that she knew in her heart what was coming for her. These words spoke volumes to both of our hearts. We did not know how long Angela's life would go on. We still had hopes that she would beat this horrible disease, but there were certainly not a lot of positive signs at the time.

As I write these words, Gianna comes to my desk and seeing the Shel Silverstein book opened to "The Clock Man," she asks, "Are you writing about The Clockman?"

"Yes, Honey, I am." I pause. "Gianna, do you remember this poem making Mommy sad?"

"Yes," she replies.

"Did you know why it made her sad? Did you know it was because she didn't want to die?"

"Yes, I knew that."

"When did you figure that out? Was it after she died?" I inquired.

"No, I knew when she read it."

"Mommy would have paid all of the pearls in all of the seas to stay with us, Gianna."

"Yeah, but she's in heaven now," she replies.

"Yes, in complete joy."

Funny thing about life is we think we have all the time in the world. We think we can go on forever, and we do not worry so much about the clock that is ticking. How much time do we really have? Do we really have days as many as smiles? We fall so much in love with this life. We act as if this life on earth is the best there is - the cake, the icing and the ice cream on the side. Yet this life is nothing compared to the eternity we have in heaven. This life is barely even some flour and eggs thrown in the bowl. Heaven, that's where life truly is. This life is a sneeze in the span of eternity. Our time here will look like seconds once we join the vastness of heaven. This life is a prelude, an opening act.

The Christian is called to live in a paradox of sorts. On the one hand, we are called to live this life with great love and fervor. Jesus tells us that He came to give us an abundant life (cf. John 10:10). We are called to live life on earth with great passion and drive, striving to be who God created us to be. As trite as it may sound, the goal of our life should be to leave this earth and those around us better than when we got here. Yet at the same time, the Christian is called to live with abandonment to this life. We are called to live with a readiness to accept our call home to heaven. We are called to live in this temporal world with the purpose of knowing that any day could be our last. It is easy to get stuck sometimes in the love of this life. It is easy to get lost in the temporal and forget the forever. Even knowing our goal of heaven, it is easy to fall in love in the many in-betweens of our journey: love of family, love of a spouse, love of a career, love of a ministry or mission, love of travel, love of adventure. All of these are good, yet none of these is the icing, none of these is the cake, not one of these compares to the greater plan God has for us.

Despite Angela's intense desire for heaven and her very real understanding that all life was about a journey to heaven, she still did not want to die. She, just like the rest of us, dreamed of a long life. We dreamed of that life together. We would quip about living until we were 100. She would say, "I'm going to be in such good shape when I'm older. We are going to be active and fit and we are going to live a long life." More than that, she was so passionate about being the best mother she could be. She so badly wanted to do it all right. While heaven was her ultimate goal, she wanted so much more time to get there.

A GRIEF OBSERVED

After finding out Angela wouldn't be eligible for any surgery and seeing her fatigue continue and her weight continue to be dangerously low, Angela and I both began to grieve separately and together. She read C.S. Lewis' A Grief Observed and remarked that she finally felt like someone put words to how she was feeling. Angela was grieving the things we had already lost, and ultimately, the reality that she may soon die. This time was difficult for both of us, but it was also very healing. As we each shared about our grief, we only grew closer and could more freely focus on loving each other and our children with whatever time we had left. As we sojourned on this road, Angela would come to points of grief in recognizing what may be to come. At each of those points, she would choose to live those remaining days with purpose, focusing so intently on our children, myself, and making lasting memories.

Knowing now that there were no surgical options and that the chemotherapy was definitely just buying us time, we adopted an attitude of living in the moment. Each day was a day to be grateful for. If it was a day at the cancer center, Angela and I would make the best of it. We felt like it was a date. We'd get there early to have coffee and breakfast, have her follow up visits, enjoy a lunch and I would sit with her, talking or working while she got her chemotherapy treatments. We actually looked forward to those days now.

We focused wholeheartedly on family time, on making memories, and doing things we wanted to do as a family. We went on day-long adventures, took lots of walks, and even took a dream trip to Disneyland. Watching Angela share Disneyland with the kids was nothing short of miraculous. Her body did not have the energy for this, but we got an electric scooter and Angela gave everything she had to make sure the time was memorable. To this day the kids and I relive that trip, and I am so grateful that God allowed us, through the help of many, to make that trip a reality. Michael Dixon, local radio personality and host of "The Bishop's Hour" on the local Immaculate Heart Radio Affiliate asked Angela, "What gives you happiness these days?" Angela's response, "Just anytime that I am awake enough to spend quality time with my kids, just the family time we have together, that's really all I live for now."

THINGS THAT LAST...

*Having a quiet moment of gratitude. Joyfully looking
forward to entering 2012, no regrets for the past...ready to
embark on the next bit of our journey, which is mostly about
our journey towards heaven. Seek ye first the kingdom of
God...alleluia!*

(Angela Faddis, December 31, 2011)

Our journey through life is not ultimately about all of the
many expectations we build up in ourselves over the years. It's
not about the great job, the perfect house, the success, the perfect
spouse, the romance, the family, the perfect number of children,
the lavish vacations, or the nest egg we build to live off of. Our
journey in life, all of it - the good, the bad, the extreme high points
of joy and bliss, along with the downright awful pain and difficulty
of loss or failure - all of it is ordered to get us to heaven. Those
things and expectations - great job, perfect house, success, the
dream spouse, the romance, the children - can certainly be a part
of our life and, properly ordered, those desires can be our path to
heaven. However, when not properly ordered, when those things
become our measure of happiness, when they become our safety
or our stronghold, they become a hindrance and obstacle on our
journey to heaven.

In this life we seem to find ourselves constantly focusing
on the temporal things of life, and often we choose those temporary things over those which last. Angela knew in her heart that
the Kingdom of Heaven was her goal. We, like most other couples,
would often dream of those temporal successes in life, but again

and again we would find ourselves turning back to the things that last. In particular, I recall our decision for me to go back to school to become a chiropractor. There were many reasons for this decision, including the need for financial stability. There was also this focus on becoming wealthy and successful that had somehow taken hold of us. Having wealth and professional success is not a bad thing; however, if this becomes our focus, our goal, it can take us far away from the path toward heaven. In the midst of this year of planning and discerning, we developed our own five or six year plan. After visiting the chiropractic school we had chosen and meeting the students who had families, we learned that in order for me to achieve this goal, I would have to sacrifice more than we were willing. I would have to sacrifice our family life and most likely, Angela would have to sacrifice staying at home. This sacrifice was too great for us, not because we were unwilling to work hard or give up pleasures in life, but because of what we knew was our real goal in life: to get each other and our children to heaven. We talked and prayed and both felt this uneasiness in our hearts. After a few weeks of discussion and deliberation, we knew clearly that we could not sacrifice our family for a career. In the end, that five-year plan would have been cut short by Angela's cancer diagnosis. Even if I was able to continue chiropractic school while Angela underwent cancer treatment, her death would have come one year before I would have finished.

"Seek ye first the kingdom of God..." (cf. Matthew 6:33). At the end of it all, would it have mattered if I had made more money, had more success, and built that dream life? In the end, she would have still died and we would have missed out on the simplicity of living for heaven. Angela knew in her heart that time was precious.

She knew that her singular focus in life was on our marriage and on caring for our children. In her seeking first the kingdom, she chose to love me and our children with great intention. By focusing on the things that matter in life, we were able to choose the things that last. And in so choosing, I can see the absolute providence of God's gentle guidance in that decision to forego our desire and trust in God's will for our lives.

That decision was also a sacrifice; we struggled to live off of one small salary, and we did not get to enjoy many of the "pleasures" of life. But in the end, Angela would say she didn't regret not having incredible vacations and material comforts; she was grateful she had so much time with our children. We made the best of what we had and filled our free time with memories and intentional time as a family. Being the one left behind to care for our children, I cannot express how grateful I am for the time Angela had with them. She loved them so intentionally over those five and a half years, and our children know without a doubt that their mother loved them in that way. In seeking first the kingdom, Angela trusted that God would get us through the lean times and the difficulty of never having enough. She also trusted that by choosing what was best for our family over the material desires of her heart, she was indeed choosing to store up treasures in heaven.

If you have a five-year plan for your life, I would encourage you to hand it over to God. It doesn't mean you have to throw it out, but to truly walk with trust, we must let God be the author of our plans. God may lead you to throw out your plan, or He may change it up a bit. Either way, I can promise you that what God hands you back will not only be His perfect will, but it will also lead to your ultimate joy. Our five-year plan would have never included Angela dying at the age of 32, but it also wouldn't have prevented that from happening either. Instead, I'd be left with a lot of regret. All those extra hours spent away from our family and all that hardship would have left me with a deep wound. It's not to say that a husband and father should not go back to school or better his career or financial situation by taking those steps. For many, this is the proper path. However, if we fail to hand those plans to God, or let Him make them before we even get involved, then we cannot listen to truly know what His will is.

We spend so much time trying to fit God into our plans or fit those things that are most important into our own desires that we often find ourselves having charted a course that is so far from where we are supposed to be that we have no clue how to get back. When we only look at ourselves - our wants, desires, goals, personal fulfillment - we often are not looking at the road ahead and the things that matter. Until we realize that the only way to find ourselves is to throw ourselves into the arms of Jesus and let Him show us the way, we will continue this constant circle of moving forward and getting lost over and over again.

To find your true self, you must first lose yourself in the love of God. It's that simple and true. God ordered it this way for a reason. We were made for Him. As St. Augustine so rightly said, "My soul is restless until it rests in you." This is God's design: we need Him. And it is not because it somehow makes Him feel good. It's not an ego trip for God. He designed us to need Him as our compass, our guide, so that we will always find our way back to Him. So when Angela and I felt this uneasiness about our plans for school and what it would do to our family, when we sat and prayed and felt this ache in our guts, it was God's way of telling us, "Hey,

I know what's coming, I know what you truly desire, and I know that you are going to regret this decision." Had we continued on that path, I'm certain God would have still been by our side and blessed our free will with His grace and mercy, but I also know that God knew the weight of pain that would have placed on us in the end. God knew that our time was precious and that what was most important was that we loved one another fully and gave everything we had to one another as spouses and to our children.

Several months before Angela died, I heard her crying in the shower and she asked me to come to the bathroom to talk. She told me that she was standing there and just thinking about how all she wanted for the kids, the only thing she cared about was that they know Jesus. She said, "I just want them to know Jesus and to know that all that matters in life is that they are close to Him." She said, "Chris, I want them to have a good life, but really I just want them to know Jesus. In the end I don't care if they are good at school or sports or anything. I just care that they know that a relationship with Christ is the most important thing. If I die, promise me they will know." We talked at great length that day, as we had before, about our desires for our children. Ultimately, Angela wanted our children to understand from the very beginning of their life that it is Jesus that matters most and that the rest of it all is nothing in comparison.

It is always a tragedy when someone young dies. It is no different with Angela. How in the world does someone like her, someone who was physically active, ate healthy, was fit most of her life, and who never had an indication of colon problems get late stage colon cancer at such a young age? We'll never know why this happened or why it was allowed to happen. I can't promise that something like this will not happen in your life either. But what I can promise is that if you continually place your life into the arms of God, if you make heaven your goal and order everything in your life towards heaven, God will lead you in the way you should go. And if your end is to come soon, at least you will know that you lived in the will of God and in so doing you will store up those treasures in heaven.

When the clock man comes, will we beg for more of this life? Or will we strive to live those precious days remaining with incredible intent and focus on the Cross? We can see in Angela's cancer journey that she certainly grieved the things of this life that she would slowly have to let go of, but she did so with an abandon to the Cross and to the promise of heaven.

I suppose we can say that as Angela surrendered those last months of her life she could have changed the words of the poem:

"How much will you pay for an extra day?"
He asked when the time came to die.
"Not one penny," the answer came,
"For heaven is all I desire."

Death Comes Knocking

A NIGHTMARE AND REALITY

"Chris, am I really here? Am I really alive?" Angela asked. It was 4 a.m. and I had heard some stumbling in the hallway. I awoke to find Angela walking around somewhat delirious and feeling her body as if she was trying to make sure she wasn't dreaming.

"Of course you are, Angela. I'm right here with you," I replied.

"But, where am I? Am I here? Am I still alive?" The look of fear and worry on her face made it clear. This was no simple nightmare. I hugged her and calmed her and walked her back to the bed. She sat there looking around as if she couldn't see me.

I said, "Angela can you see me? Can you hear my voice?"

"Yes, yes I can hear you, but I feel like you are far away," she replied. "I can see you, but it's like I'm looking at you and I'm not here."

For the next hour she would continue to feel her body and ask questions, begging me to talk so she could know she was still there. I talked and prayed with her for nearly an hour and though she calmed, the overwhelming sense that she was not present didn't dissipate. While she was delirious, she was able to clearly talk about her fears and worries. "I need more time," she said. "I'm not ready yet."

"Need more time for what?" I inquired.

"I'm not holy enough yet. I'm not done, I have more to do, I am not holy enough," she repeated.

I encouraged her, "Angela, God will make you holy. When it's your time to go, God will make you holy; He will make all things new." Finally after a long while, she decided to try and watch a show to fall asleep. She woke up a few hours later, feeling normal.

It was now early August and she had just returned from the hospital only a couple of days earlier. On that visit we learned that her chemotherapy was no longer working, and the cancer had started to spread again. She also had a very large amount of fluid buildup that was causing great discomfort and some possible infections. Chemotherapy was not an option until we got some of these things under control. She was in the hospital for about two weeks during which she had several procedures done, including some very painful procedures to drain her kidneys and put in a drain port for the fluid buildup in her abdomen. This visit was the most frightening and difficult for us. Angela and I had very somber conversations, and while we wouldn't say it, I think we both knew that the end could be near. Once they were able to get some of her symptoms under control, we were sent home and were hopeful that within a week or two they could get her started on the clinical trial that had been suggested. Upon returning home, Angela's fatigue only worsened and her fluid buildup and other symptoms did not seem to improve.

It was only a few days after returning home from the hospital that Angela woke up with this out of body experience. She also had some other dreams about death that week, and this experience was telling for me. I just knew that this meant something. We began to talk again about death, about what it would mean, and in a sense, began to prepare each other for what we both knew in our hearts was coming next. I learned through some reading and some conversations that this experience was not all that uncommon among the terminally ill as they approached death.

A few days later we returned to the Cancer Treatment Center for an appointment with the counselor to discuss Angela's nightmare and for her to process all that she was sensing and feeling. Her drain tube was causing a great deal of pain, and so we headed in early. As the team in the internal medicine clinic tried to help her with her pain, it became clear Angela was not only in a great deal of pain, but she was also not doing well at all. We didn't make it to that counseling appointment; instead, Angela was admitted.

Angela had been checked into the hospital numerous times for pain or infection, but this visit was very different. We all knew it. There is a photo that I posted to Facebook that day of Augustine holding Angela's hand as she lies in pain waiting to be admitted. It speaks volumes of the understanding we all had that day of her situation. Gianna and Augustine were beginning to show their sadness, and they were really beginning to see Angela's suffering in a way that they had likely been shielded from before. Though she didn't say it, there was a certain tone to Angela's voice and an awareness in her eyes that this time things were different. The next few days would hold many procedures and talks with specialists.

Her pain was becoming unmanageable and it became clear to her physicians that she may need some new pain medication. Her fluid buildup was also hard to manage and draining her abdomen daily didn't seem to be doing the trick. Three days into her visit, there was a concern about some discharge from her feeding tube site. A CT scan was ordered to rule out a few possible causes. The CT scan didn't reveal anything regarding the drainage, but it did tell us something we had feared.

THE END DRAWS NEAR

It was Friday, August 10, and that night I was planning to take the kids home and stay with them. As we were leaving Angela's room, the hospitalist called me over to tell me that the radiologist called. The CT scan he said shows some very aggressive growth. I was told to prepare for the worst. It wasn't his call as he wasn't our oncologist, but from what he knew, he said Angela was likely nearing the end. I went back in to her room to give her another kiss, knowing that I couldn't tell her what I was just told quite yet. She was very tired and needed rest, and I wanted and needed time to think. I pressed my lips on her forehead and held her in that moment. Death had come knocking, and while I knew this moment was likely coming, I wasn't ready.

We had spoken of death a great deal in the months leading up to this. Angela and I both talked about our grief. We let go of each other little by little as Angela's fatigue worsened. I recall one conversation we had where I explained to Angela that I felt I was losing a piece of her every day. One of the hardest things for me was when she could no longer stay awake after the kids went to bed. We always stayed up together for a couple of hours after they went to sleep, and on many nights, we enjoyed a glass of wine and sometimes a little chocolate. That part of us had already been laid to rest. Angela grieved as well. Having read C.S. Lewis' A Grief Observed, Angela shared publicly, "It is mind blowing. Like he looked inside my mind and soul and wrote what he saw - what I haven't been able to put into words. Want to know why I don't write much? It's because I can't do it justice...my thoughts, feelings are too complex... I have to say it sure is a relief to know that Lewis suffered the way I am suffering." Lewis expressed what she couldn't. This helped Angela and I to grieve together as it gave her the words to share her pain with me.

So the words the doctor spoke, they were not unexpected or surprising. So much was pointing to this possibility, but to hear them? To know the time was coming, that death was knocking? The "Clockman" had come to call again and I was not ready; I was numb and all I could do was kiss her and hold her a moment longer. The look in her eyes told me she knew that there was a reason for this long goodbye, but she was gracious and just loved me and said goodnight, not inquiring more.

The night was long. I took the kids home, called a few of those closest to us and tried to sleep. At around 4 a.m. I woke up to my phone ringing. It was Angela calling from the hospital. She said she couldn't sleep and was feeling restless. We talked for a minute and I knew something else was going on. I said, "Honey, are you okay? Is something upsetting you?"

She began to cry, though she tried to hold it in. "I had a dream," she said. "Dad had come for a visit; he came in October, but it was too late. He was too late. I was already gone."

"Oh Angela, I'm so sorry," I replied, holding back the tears myself.

"Chris, am I going to die soon?"

"Angela, I don't know how much time is left, but it isn't looking very good." We spoke for a few more minutes about her dream and what it meant. I didn't want to tell her about the CT scan over the phone and I also knew that what I was told wasn't complete until we got further information. I said, "Angela, if you are feeling like you need your dad to come here, and if you fear it'll be too late, then I think we have to get him here. I will call him first thing in the morning."

She said, "I want him here."

I asked her if there was anyone else she needed to see, and she asked for two of her best friends. I called them in the morning as well.

The next day was filled with visitors as Angela had asked to see friends and family that weekend. It was non-stop guests all day long. None of the visitors knew what I knew. Also, because the visits were back-to-back, I never really had the time to share with Angela what was going on. My heart was heavy and everyone could tell. At one point, when two of her girlfriends, Melanie Hart and Melanie Pritchard were painting her nails and giving her a pedicure, I looked down at her ankles. The day before I had noticed some severe swelling in Angela's back. I was told it was the fluid buildup – known as edema - and was fairly par for the course. It was a sign of her decline. When I saw her ankles, I immediately began to cry. Seeing her like this was so difficult. After a while we asked for a break for Angela, and everyone left the room. As I got her up to the restroom and then helped her settle in for a nap, she gave me a loving and concerned look. She asked if I was okay and I gave a simple yes. She inquired with a simple look of her eyes. She said no words, but when you love someone for so long, you tend to learn what a look means.

So I said, "Do you want to know what's happening?"

"Yes I do," she replied, "I can tell you are not okay."

So I told her what I was told the night before. She wasn't surprised and didn't say a whole lot. We held each other, and I cried. She cried too, but it was clear her concern in this moment was for me. After some time, she rested and I went back to our friends and family.

After sharing with family and friends what was happening and spending more time with Angela that evening, we decided to share the news publicly. With a broken heart, I shared the following message that Sunday morning:

My heart is heavy. These last few days have been grueling, overwhelming and hard to swallow. Angela's condition has worsened. We do not know all of the details and will not know until we see an oncologist tomorrow, but her tumors are growing and I'm told they are being very aggressive. Without a whole lot to report, the on call doc told me to prepare for bad news.

Angela is alert though foggy due to pain meds. Her pain continues to increase. The fluid from her tumors is now throughout her body. I noticed Friday that her back began to swell and then her legs yesterday and now her ankles and feet. While this in and of itself is not threatening, it is a sign of the continued progression of the cancer.

Tomorrow we will meet with her team of docs and get guidance on next steps. We are hoping that they still have some things they can do.

This time is very difficult, but Angela is handling it with great faith. Thank you for your continued prayers.

The next day we met with Angela's oncology team and a palliative care physician to discuss her options. The bottom line was that chemotherapy would kill her at this stage, and the only way treatment could be an option was if the fluid buildup was under control. However, it was clear that the buildup was anything but under control. Angela asked several questions, and the team was very gracious with helping us understand. The recommendation was that we get Angela's pain under control and transition to hospice care, though we were also given the option of staying at the hospital as long as Angela wanted.

The team left the room and Angela and I sat in the silence and solitude of that moment. Her words were something I'll never forget: "You mean I'm not going to get a medical miracle? You mean I'm not going to ever get up and put on a pair of running shoes and run this cancer away?" Shortly after Angela's diagnosis she read a story about a woman who got cancer and instead of getting treatment, she put on a pair of running shoes and began to run; she became an avid runner and literally ran herself back to health. The cancer never came back. Angela had always hoped to get healthy enough and strong enough to do just that. Now it was clearly too late. My response to her was simply, "No one can say you won't get a miracle. That's God's business, and we are not giving up on that. But medically, there's just nothing they can do. So all we have left is prayer." We laid in that hospital bed together weeping. Our hearts broken, there was little comfort we could offer one another. There was no shielding each other from the reality that lie before us. I was certainly tempted to explain it away or to offer some solace with empty words of promises I could not keep. I think we often do this: "Oh it will all work out. Surely God won't let you die. Surely a miracle is coming." Truth is, I believed fully in the possibility of a miracle, but I also knew I wasn't in the business of making that promise. Regardless, I had to allow her the mercy to grieve, to feel the pain, to suffer, even though every single part of me wished I could ease this pain.

We had several conversations that night and in the coming days. Angela again said, "I'm not ready to die. I need more time. I'm not holy enough." I again said, "God will make you holy; you only need to ask Him. He will make you ready." Over the coming days, Angela's pain was evident as she lamented leaving this place. Yet every time she lamented, cried, or shared her pain, she would always point back to God. One night, she said, "I want to be here to see my children grow up. I want to be there to teach Gianna about boys and to help her understand how important it is that she be treated right. I want to be there to see her go to prom and graduate. I want to watch Augustine learn to drive and see him become a man. I want to be there for their 18th birthdays. I just want more time. I just don't understand why I can't have more time." A short while later she shared, "You know, I've had a great life. I've been to so many incredible places. I've experienced things that most people never will. I have always had great people in my life. No matter where I've lived, God has always blessed me with incredible friends. He gave me two amazing children. I have a husband who cherishes me. I've had an incredible life. But all of that is about me. I guess it's not really about me anymore. It's about God." Though Angela would lament much more over the next few days, this example demonstrates the incredible depth of her faith; even when she couldn't understand why this was happening and even when it was hardest to let go, she would simply offer it back to God. Her lament turned into a beautiful prayer of praise.

Over the next week we would take lots of visitors, including our friend, Father John Parks, who came to anoint Angela and spend some time with her. Knowing she wanted to have some time alone to talk to him, I took the kids and left for a while. We thought an hour was enough time but when we came back, they were still talking. Two hours later, Father Parks came out and said, "You married an incredible woman. Truly, she is unbelievable." I would find out later that Father Parks felt as though she was ministering to him. He would later tell a mutual friend that this visit was probably the most powerful two hours of his priesthood. I recall Angela seeming renewed when I came back to the room; she was refreshed and had a new energy about her.

Angela's family and friends began coming into town during that last week at the hospital, including her father and her two best friends that she requested to see. Though Angela was still mourning, it was a big boost to have so many loved ones near during this time. She was tired but welcomed the company. We shared lots of memories and many tears, but the laughs were abundant. Our family joined us for the rosary a few times, friends Dave and Alice Burba came and led us in prayerful song, and many people came to entertain our children.

Doctors worked to get Angela's pain under control and put her on a protocol we could manage from home. We still had yet to make the call to go home. This of course seemed to be the most obvious course of action, but Angela felt a little worried about leaving the incredible care of CTCA. She felt so comfortable there and felt as though she was getting the best care she could receive. We discussed it at length several times. Finally, she said to me, "It just feels so strange, as if I'm going home to die." It made sense now, the hesitation, as if going home meant giving up. In truth, it meant nothing more than choosing where she would like to die. She had already agreed that she felt it would be better for her, as well as for the kids and me, if we were home, but choosing to go home was clearly hard for her. I paused for a bit and then thought about something one of the doctors had told me about people having much more vitality at home. In many cases people lived a lot longer after going home than if they stayed in the hospital. "Angela," I said, "Let's not go home to die. Let's go home so you can live whatever time you have left in our home with the kids and me and all our loved ones by your side. Let's go home to your dream neighborhood and the house you love." She smiled. "Maybe," I said, "it'll be like Dr. Estrada said and you'll rebound and have more vitality and you'll live longer than we think!" With a grin on her face – the same grin that always told me when something resonated with her heart – she replied, "Okay, I will go home to live. I can go home to live."

With that, we settled on going home. Hospice representatives came to meet with us, and we made arrangements to head home in the next few days. I asked Angela how she wanted things to be set up at home. She said she would like to be in our bedroom, and she would like to have our room redone in gray with pops of deep purple and white. She wanted black and white photos from our wedding near our bed, and she wanted to have the kids in the room with her. I called upon the Harts, our dear friends, and they coordinated everything. Our friends, Beth and Josh, donated the paint and the Harts, Avenzinis, and Heaths spent the weekend redecorating our bedroom. My brother James was tasked with finishing the paint downstairs in the colors Angela had wanted for a long time. The hospice bed arrived just before we did and was placed in a nook in our room. Above the bed were several wedding photos and across the room was a photo of the Virgin Mary and some other photos and statues. It was beautiful, tranquil, and everything Angela dreamed.

As we got ready to leave the hospital, many of the staff began to come in to say their goodbyes. It was clear this was very difficult, as many of them came in and were fighting back tears. As they turned away from her, they would begin to cry. Their hugs with Angela and me expressed their sorrow. Later some of them would tell me that they lose people all the time, but Angela was different, that there was something about her that they all connected with. I made my rounds that morning to say goodbye and thank you to the countless staff that took such incredible care of Angela and our entire family during our time there.

While we were so heavily focused on what was going on in the hospital, outside the hospital an incredible thing was happening. Angela's story was spreading around the world in an incredible way. Her Facebook page, which we had used since early on to update supporters and prayer warriors, had grown from around 2,000 followers to close to 6,000. It would eventually grow to over

7,000. People were sharing Angela's plight and our prayer requests all over the world. Just like when Angela was first diagnosed, a ground swell of support came in as we received emails, Facebook comments, letters, and cards from around the world. Convents again were praying; churches around the country were offering special Masses or services; and online bloggers and podcasters, along with radio hosts, were sharing Angela's story. A Catholic radio host, blogger and podcaster Gary Zimak shared our story and called upon other Catholics to join him in offering for Angela a virtual spiritual bouquet in the form of Hail Marys and rosaries offered. All told, he eventually collected close to 30,000 Hail Marys. He also hosted a live rosary for Angela and shared her story on a very popular nationally syndicated radio show. Twitter and Facebook were abuzz with people sharing our story, and the heartfelt prayers for a miracle gave our weary souls hope. It was, again, as if the people of God were acting as a shelter for us from this storm.

Death had come knocking, and we were most certainly disheartened, but death could not steal our faith, our hope, and our joy. Angela, though hurting and struggling with accepting this all, was ready to go home and live; she knew it was only a matter of time before she would have to surrender to God.

Surrender with Joy

*"You are not living for yourself but for souls, and other souls
will profit from your sufferings. Your prolonged suffering
will give them the light and strength to accept My will"*

(Divine Mercy in My Soul, 67)

I WANT THE WORLD TO KNOW

"Angela, I want you to know that your body is showing
signs that you will die soon." Angela's palliative care physician,
Christine, who treated her at CTCA and also worked for the
hospice that we chose, wanted to help prepare Angela for what was
to come. We had been home from the hospital for a few days, and
Christine came to check on Angela. She had examined Angela
and, after taking me in the hallway to let me know what she was
seeing, she wanted to share some insight with Angela to prepare
her and alleviate any fears. What Christine saw in her evaluation
were some further signs of the pre-active dying process. According
to her prognosis, Angela probably only had four to six days left.
She continued, "In the next couple of days, you will start to feel a
lot more sleepy and tired; you will sleep a lot, and eventually you

won't wake up much, and you will simply slip away. I want you to know that this will be peaceful and painless. I don't want you to be scared. Angela, you will slip away and the vastness of a love that is greater than ours will take you home."

Angela listened to Christine very attentively with a slight smile, and when Christine was finished she replied to her, "I have a lot of people to pray for when I get to heaven." I was a little taken aback by her response, not because I disbelieved it, but because I expected more grief or perhaps more questions. We had been home for only a few days at this point and things were very busy with getting the kids situated and having lots of guests. With Angela sleeping so much of the time, we honestly didn't really get to talk since we had been home. The last conversations we had at the hospital about her death were still sad and filled with such grief.

After a few moments I walked Christine out to her car. As I headed back in to our bedroom, I was still feeling concerned that Angela would be very sad. I came in and my mom had just spent a few minutes with Angela. She looked a bit surprised, and she told me that Angela told her she was going to die soon, but that she was at peace with it. I came into the room and sat by Angela's bed. She gave me a look of love with a slight grin. I said, "Are you okay? How are you feeling?" She looked me in the eye and said, "I am okay, and I am at peace with it." She continued, "I want the world to know that no matter what, they must trust in Jesus, no matter what." Here she was, the one who was surrendering to death, the one who needed to be consoled, and instead she was consoling me. Asking my mother further what Angela said to her, this is what she shared: "I want people to know that no matter what, they must trust in Jesus. Even when I could not say the words, I knew I had to trust in Jesus and I would ask Chris to say the words with me. He held my hand and said, "Jesus, I trust in You." Only a few days earlier, Angela was still lamenting her death, and while she certainly turned it to God every time, this response was a marked difference. It was clear that in those few days Angela had begun to truly surrender to God.

TELLING THE CHILDREN

We decided that afternoon that it was time to tell our two children that she was dying. The weekend, being so full of guests, was not really a good time for us, so we decided to tell them on Monday. I dreaded this moment for so long and now it was here. On the one hand, I so badly wanted to tell them that Angela only had a few weeks to live, and on the other, I wanted so badly to protect them from it. I was a wreck the entire day, but Angela was completely peaceful. A few people had brought by books for the kids – books about heaven, about grief and the like. We had read a couple of those ahead for this conversation, which proved to be helpful.

The time came and I called Gianna and Augustine into our room; they sat with Angela and I sat on the bed across from her. I had thought through this moment over and over again. I thought about different ways to say it and as we tend to do, I tried to think of ways to soften the blow, to make it hurt less. But the reality was, it didn't matter what I said or how I said it. I was about to shatter their world in a few short words, and the only thing I could really do was be prepared for whatever response they had.

I began the conversation by talking about how sick

Mommy was and how we all hoped she would get better, but that she wasn't getting better. Then, trying my hardest not to cry, I told them that Mommy was not going to get better and that she was going to die soon. I don't remember my exact phrasing, but that was the gist. Both kids immediately reacted. Augustine with a cry, Gianna by getting angry. With tears streaming down our faces, we just held them there. Angela was quiet and allowed me to calm them and say what needed to be said. After some time, Angela spoke to them about how much she loved them and how she didn't want to leave them, but her body was too sick; she had to surrender to God and it was time for her to go to heaven. We talked about heaven, about where Angela would be. Our approach with our children has always been to tell them the most basic version of things and let them ask the questions they need to ask in order to understand better. They asked a couple of questions, and then they were done. They were both still pretty upset, but they didn't want to keep talking about it. Augustine laid in bed with Angela awhile, and Gianna went to the playroom. She asked me if I could read one of her books about heaven. I did, and I could see her really thinking it through. Augustine didn't want to hear about heaven – after all, heaven was taking his mother from him.

This was about as difficult an afternoon as you can imagine, but it was also so much less difficult than I thought. That day we had received a package from an organization named the St. Gianna Physician's Guild, named after our Gianna's namesake - St. Gianna. St. Gianna died in the 60's and is the first working mother to be named a saint. Her children are still alive, including her youngest daughter, Gianna Emanuela. St. Gianna carried Gianna Emanuela to term despite recommendations to terminate the birth due to cancer. The founder of the physician's guild had heard Angela's story through a friend of ours, and he personally asked Gianna Emanuela to pray for our family. Her response: "I will take this prayer to my saint-mother's grave." We had told our Gianna this story and her heart was so warmed to know that her saint's daughter was praying for her. After reading the heaven book, Gianna asked to watch the video about St. Gianna that came in her package. After watching the video that night, Gianna talked about how her Mommy might be a saint just like St. Gianna.

That afternoon Gianna told me she really wanted to make a picture for Angela. The next morning, I set her up at our dining table with paints and paper. Family was on duty while I went for a short walk to think; I came home and Gianna had painted an incredible picture, and she gave it to her mother with great joy. Over the coming weeks many would comment on the picture, some saying it looked like stained glass, others like a doorway to heaven, others that it reminded them of the coloring of the image of Our Lady of Guadalupe. It was clear that this gift was of Gianna's heart, and it was her goodbye to Angela.

Augustine's response was different, most definitely more reflective and melancholic. He didn't want to talk about it much and vacillated between wanting to be lying in bed with Angela and not wanting to be near her. His heart was surely broken and he said many times, "I don't want Mommy to die and go to heaven!" The next day he asked if he could go into Mommy's room. He had several toys with him. He said he was going to work on Mommy. I watched as he tenderly and lovingly checked on her and "worked" on her. It was clear he was trying to help her get better. Angela looked at him with such love and thanked him. This was

Augustine' way to share his sadness and love with his mother. If no one else could fix her, he felt he should try.

Tuesday came and Angela was very fatigued and showed more signs of decline. It seemed Christine was right, though Angela would find these bursts of energy and I'd find her trying to get out of bed. She wanted to spend time with the kids and so I carried her downstairs so she could lie on the couch. That night, after putting the kids down and getting Angela situated, my dad came over to spend time with me. He brought a little whiskey and some wings, and our plan was to drown our sorrows so to speak. We made ourselves each a drink, got situated outside, and I set up the monitor so I could hear Angela upstairs. Two minutes later, I heard panting and grunting sounds. I dropped everything and sprinted upstairs. I found Angela struggling for breath and going into what seemed to be a cardiac arrest. She was writhing and trying to fight back. I was aware this was possible and immediately began giving her the medication she needed and contacted hospice. Angela was gasping and then simply could not breathe, though she was still fighting back and trying. It was a horrific sight; it was everything Angela feared about death. It was clear she was not ready to go, and I was not going to let her go like this. I simply wanted to calm this episode, assuming that she would still go quickly. I just wanted her to go in peace. When her breathing finally stopped and it seemed she was about to go, I began giving her chest compressions. I gave her a few breaths of mouth-to-mouth and she began to breathe again, but was still in what is known as "terminal restlessness." Essentially, her eyes were open but she couldn't see or hear us and was non-responsive, and she was moving her arms and legs as if to walk or run away. Doctors describe this state as similar to when you have a dream where you are about to fall off of a cliff, but you wake up. I called the doctor, and she gave me instructions on how to calm her episode and get her to a resting state. This was a sign that she would go very soon. Christine told me that she was not likely to regain consciousness and explained that her pulses would probably disappear soon. At that point, she would probably live about four to six hours. It took a while for Angela to calm, but she did finally calm. In between giving her medication, I prayed. A couple hours into this episode, she regained consciousness and slowly was able to see us and recognize us. She didn't say a lot of words, but she talked a little and was able to answer our questions. The on-call hospice nurse arrived and did not expect Angela to be conscious. She checked her out and made sure we had what we needed, but she was very surprised Angela was awake. She explained further what could happen and what I should expect, and then she went home. We got Angela calm and began treating her with a little oxygen to help her rest that night. I posted a message to Facebook letting everyone know that she was likely within her last hours and the prayers were again poured out in full force. The next morning, Angela showed no further signs of decline, and while she slept a lot and was not very talkative, she seemed to have rebounded.

It became clear at this point that Angela was no longer living for herself. She was becoming resigned to this life. There was a sense of detachment that I could feel and see in her. It was as if she had greater things on her mind now. We would talk about the kids and me moving forward after she died, and she would say, "Promise me you will follow through on the things God has called you to, and I know you and the kids will be okay." I would tell her a story about one of the kids and she would smile a loving smile, but I could just tell she had let go of us. At one point, I asked her about this and she said, "I know God will take care of you."

As people came to see her and, in a sense, say their goodbyes, Angela was more focused on being there for them and comforting them. She would have long conversations with some, sharing stories and wisdom. People would leave her room and say things like, "There is so much peace and joy in that room." Angela's college friend, a transitional Deacon at the time, Gaurav Schroff (now Father Gaurav Schroff), came for a very short visit to see her. I was in the room for a time while he visited, and it was incredible to hear him share with Angela how her faith during college was a tremendous witness to him and had a big impact on his own faith and his priesthood. He spent a good chunk of the day with her and upon leaving shared that he came to minister to her, but it was clear she was ministering to him. He and others described entering Angela's room like being on holy ground.

When I came across this quote from St. Faustina a few days later, it was the perfect description of what was happening in Angela. The words came from St. Faustina's diary and they are an account of what Jesus said to her while she was in great suffering: "You are not living for yourself but for souls, and other souls will profit from your sufferings. Your prolonged suffering will give them the light and strength to accept My will" (Divine Mercy in My Soul, 67).

The day after Angela nearly died, she shared that she was seeing lots of people. It was a day with few visitors, so I was confused. I said "Do you mean our family and friends who have come by to visit?"

"No," she replied, "not them. I see lots of other people."

"Do you mean like the angels and saints?" I inquired.

"I think so," Angela replied.

I asked her, "Angela, are you talking to God or to the angels and saints?"

"Yes, I think so," she replied.

I tried to inquire about what she was saying or what they were saying. She only said that this was all making sense now. Later I asked her, "Angela, when you're talking to God, have you mentioned to God that your husband sure would like it if you could stay?" I, of course, asked this as a joke.

She laughed as she replied, "No, but they did tell me I would be healed completely body and soul." She turned her head and went back to sleep.

I sat there thinking to myself, "Wow, I guess it is really her time to go; who am I to stop her?" I immediately assumed that she had meant she would be healed when she got to heaven, but later that day I got to thinking that maybe she did mean a miracle. The next day, I asked her about this conversation again. "Angela, do you remember telling me that you were told you'd be healed completely body and soul?"

"Yes, I do. That's what they told me."

"So, can I ask you, did they mean healed completely in heaven or did they mean on earth, like a miracle?"

She laughed a little and looked at me with a sweet smile, putting her hand to my chest, "I'm pretty sure they meant in heaven. But I could be wrong. Either way, what does it matter? I'll be whole again."

When I married Angela, I did so with the knowledge that

my job was to help her get to heaven. Here I sat with her, just a few feet from our marriage bed, and she was at the doorway of heaven. Who was I to keep her from the one place she's always wanted to be, and the place I promised to help her get to? She was ready to go, and while it seemed that God was keeping her around for some purpose, it was clear it wasn't for her. Perhaps it was for us, for those of us who loved her so dearly, or perhaps it was for souls, especially for the many praying for her. As Jesus said to St. Faustina, "Your prolonged suffering will give them the light and strength to accept My will."

AN ACT OF MERCY

That day I got word that a family member had come into town despite Angela's request that she not come. After this person repeatedly hurt Angela and me, Angela had cut off ties with her a few years earlier. Angela had sought counseling and prayed about this a great deal and felt it was best for her and for our family if this person not be a part of our lives. She also forgave her and worked on healing from the pain of this relationship. Angela told me at the hospital, "I've already forgiven her and I don't need to see her. I just don't see the point, it will just cause me more pain and I've let it go." After hearing Angela would not see her, she wrote a note to apologize for the hurt she had caused, something that Angela had wanted for a long time. Angela still felt she didn't need to see her, but wrote her a note saying, "I really appreciate your letter. I want you to know that I forgave you a long time ago and was never holding a grudge. It means a lot for me to see you apologize. Those were words I have needed to hear for a long time. This would have been the first step in a long road of healing. I hope you will continue this for yourself. Someday we will be reunited in heaven." Angela again made it clear that a visit was not desired, but still she came. I did not handle this well and was insistent that I would respect Angela's wishes. The hospice team and the doctor agreed and said it would be detrimental to Angela's health. I also spoke with Father Parks, who had spoken with Angela at length about this, and he agreed that I was in the right to make this decision. That night I was restless and frustrated.

Late that night I got a text from my friend, Mark, with whom I had spoken to that day about the situation: "I can't sleep and I can't stop thinking about this. If you're up, let's talk." I called him and we talked at length. Something in Mark's prayer was telling him that maybe there was a reason she was here. He agreed that this was not for Angela; it had been very clear to those of us close to Angela that she truly had forgiven and let go of the pain of this situation, but perhaps it was for the family member's own healing. Angela had written to her that she hoped that she would seek healing and that she hoped to someday reunite with her in heaven. As Mark said, "Maybe this mercy is what she needs, to hear from Angela that she is forgiven and to say goodbye." I was still struggling with the idea of going against Angela's wishes. I was her husband, and it was my job to honor her and protect her during this time. Mark lovingly encouraged me that while it was certainly my job to do so, perhaps there was something greater at hand here and God was asking me to open the door to true healing.

After an hour-long conversation we prayed for the Holy Spirit to guide my decision. I sat up and prayed a Divine Mercy

Chaplet and asked the Lord to speak into my heart. I went to sleep, and when I woke up the decision was made. She would be able to come say goodbye to Angela. I arranged for Mark and his wife to come and be present. I also would be in the room as well as two other family members. I asked someone to take Gianna and Augustine for an hour and the stage was set. I was still not at peace about it, so I sat again and prayed for a while. I went to Angela's bedside just a few minutes before she was to arrive to tell her what was happening. I simply said, "Angela, she came into town even though you said you did not want her to. I made it clear I was going to respect your wishes and was not going to let her in, but last night Mark called and we prayed about it, and I feel that maybe you need to give her this one last act of mercy."

We talked for a few moments and she looked at me and said, "Okay, she can come. Will you be here?" she asked.

"Yes, if you want me to," I responded. "I also asked Mark and Melanie to be here if you want."

She smiled and said, "Yes, I want you all here." Mark and Mel arrived a little early and came up to pray with us. Through tears, they led an absolutely beautiful prayer. My frustration and anger dissipated and Angela's face shone with incredible color. She sat up and waited for her to arrive.

Mark and Melanie can attest that the room was filled with an incredible peace as she entered the room. Angela's family member bent over her almost as if to bend to the mercy that was present. Much of their words were not heard, but I do recall hearing Angela say with great love, "I never didn't forgive you; I always forgave you, but you kept hurting me and I just couldn't allow you to hurt us anymore. Of course I forgive you." The conversation continued for ten minutes, and Angela continued to offer her love and mercy in every word. It was an incredible sight as Angela, who for much of the last three days was sleeping and couldn't stay awake for more than a few minutes at a time, was alert, attentive and confident in her words. She spoke truth with great love and the mercy was palpable. Through her offering this act of mercy, a soul was set free. Angela, too, could now let go. Though Angela knew she had forgiven her and felt at peace, she did often wonder if she could have done more. Now that she had faced this person and shown her the love and mercy that she needed, she could release it all.

Just as others had shared that they felt such a powerful presence of peace and joy in the room when they came to see Angela, it was incredible to witness how through prayer, God transformed a situation of such pain into a beautiful time of mercy. I know this because even my heart changed in this time. My hurt, anger and frustration also left me during this visit and I felt, for the first time in a long while, love for this family member. Surely, it was Jesus' Divine Mercy that allowed this moment to occur and it was that same mercy that humbled my heart to let go of my protective instincts to allow His mercy to work.

They shared a hug and she left the house. Mark, Melanie and I stayed back and Angela let out a sigh – almost as if to release it all. She was still glowing but clearly exhausted. We prayed again, and I held Angela's hand tightly. I looked to Angela after this prayer and I said, "All of the pain that was caused by that situation is now redeemed in this moment; you gave her mercy and you allowed the door for healing to be opened." She smiled at me and I held her hand again even tighter. I supposed that this moment was the reason Angela rebounded from that episode a couple of nights before.

That weekend, many family and friends would again come to visit and the stories of how she was changing them continued. I would walk in the room to see people in tears while Angela smiled and spoke. They prayed with her, sang with her and some simply sat in silence while she slept. My mom and aunts said they just wanted to stay in the room because it was like being on a retreat. It was around this time that my neighbor from across the courtyard came over to me and pointed out that we had countless butterflies circling our house. They didn't seem to go anywhere else. I watched for them, and she was right. They literally just flew back and forth by our bedroom and to the front of the house.

Something else was beginning to happen. The day after Angela nearly died I shared, "I asked Angela today if she felt the thousands of prayers and she said yes. I also asked her to remember all of you when she comes into heaven and to pray for each of you by name." Shortly after that post I began to get messages from people and realized people's prayers for Angela began to work in the opposite way. They were pleading with God for a miracle for Angela, yet God was giving them miracles in their own lives instead. One message from a complete stranger brought tears to my eyes: "You have touched me so much that I went to Mass for the first time in years. I cried the whole time." I wrote in a post telling of this message: "Angela's desire is for all to know God and trust in Him with everything. Truly her suffering is worth this one soul coming home to God." A text message that week from a close friend exclaimed, "My sister went back to church after years because of Angela. She's changing people." Another friend emailed me the same day: "My sister has not been to Mass in over fifteen years and this Sunday she went with my mom and dad. It's because she has been praying for Angela."

More strangers began to send emails telling me, "I'm sorry that Angela is not getting a miracle, but a miracle is happening in my life." The miracles came in the form of many people going back to the Church or even finding faith for the first time. One woman told me that neither she nor her husband had been to church since childhood and had never been to church together; that weekend they were beginning the search for a church to attend. Months later, she followed up to say they were still going. Others were finding healing from depression, anxiety and other mental ailments, and some were even claiming miracles of the medical sort.

Shortly after I shared this unexpected response, blogger Gary Zimak – the same blogger who organized a national prayer/rosary campaign for Angela and shared about her on the radio and podcasts – wrote us: "Angela and Chris, while I was at Mass this morning, this thought came to me. We've been praying for a healing and we've gotten many of them. Sometimes it's actually the "healthy" who need to be healed. Thank you for teaching us so much by your example. God Bless!" Gary wrote a beautiful blog telling of these unexpected miracles:

Although remaining open to the Will of God, I have been praying for a complete miraculous healing for Angela. While the Lord may still bring about that physical healing, an unexpected phenomenon is taking place. Although Angela has not been healed of her cancer, many people who are praying for her are being healed. What's interesting is that many of them didn't even realize that they were sick!

As Christians, we know that Jesus can heal the sick. We've seen many instances of this in the Bible and in our own lives. What we need to learn, however, is who the sick really are. Many times those who are seemingly healthy are the ones most in need of healing. Spiritual sickness is much worse than physical sickness because it can affect our salvation. Although we are saddened when we look at the Faddis family's situation, much good is coming out of it.

Through her illness, this brave young woman is teaching us the value of redemptive suffering. From her bed, she is instructing us in a way that far surpasses anything that can be found in a textbook. By accepting his wife's illness, Chris Faddis is reminding each of us that faith involves looking past the difficulties of life and trusting that the Lord has a better plan.

One day when Angela was lucid enough, I shared some letters and cards she had received from old friends. As I read each letter, we would chat about the friend who sent it and then move on to the next. Then I shared some of the stories I was hearing of miracles. I asked her if she liked hearing these affirmations of what she has meant to others. She gave a very joyful and peaceful smile and said yes. I said, "When I read these, I hear 'Well done, good and faithful servant.'" She replied with a simple smile and nod. I felt like I needed to affirm her and let her know what good her prayers and suffering were doing. I wanted her to know that there was a purpose in this pain, but she seemed so detached from the need to know. On one hand, it was as if she already knew; when I would tell a story of a miracle it almost seemed like she had heard it already. On the other hand, it was as if she had greater things on her mind. I know her reward will be greater than anything I could say to her. Still, it felt good for this husband to have the privilege of sharing these words with her.

SURRENDER WITH JOY

On September 7, I got a call from an old friend, Tom Booth. Tom is a Catholic musician who writes beautiful and prayerful music for the liturgy and prayer. Angela and I had seen Tom and his band only weeks before her diagnosis in Greensboro, North Carolina. In fact, Angela would say that seeing Tom in concert and praying with him was in her eyes a preparation for what was to come. "It was like a mini-retreat to get me ready," she would share. Tom was coming to town from Tucson and was going to be near my house leading a women's retreat. He wanted to know if he could come see Angela.

That afternoon, Tom arrived to a very quiet home. It was actually the quietest and most peaceful day in a while. He hugged Angela and began chatting with her as he sat in a chair and got out his guitar. Angela sat up a bit and smiled big when Tom came in the room. He asked her if he could pray with her and play for her and she said, "Of course!"

As they chatted Tom looked at Angela and said, "So I'm about to lead this retreat for eighty women tonight and I want to know – what would you say to them? You give the retreat." Realizing something powerful was about to happen, I quickly pulled out my phone and started to record Angela's words.

Her reply was beautiful: "I think even before we got our diagnosis, we were always on this path, this journey of understanding that nothing we do is in our control. And then after the diagnosis, it was just like, 'Wow! it's even more obvious; we really have no say.' It seems like everything we do is surrendering to God and His will with joy."

Tom followed Angela's words sharing, "You said you were already on that path. That's always been my impression of you guys. It's the same path. I remember seeing you in Greensboro. I've said to people, 'Yeah, I mean sometimes illness brings some to surrender.' I hadn't even talked to you yet, and I've always told people, 'No, they were already surrendering.' I think that's why you are touching so many lives, all over the country, people you don't even know." Tom began to play the song, "Here I Am," and the peace in the room was more than palpable. Angela rested and smiled, and the kids came in and out of the room praying along. Tom played a few more songs, and then he left. Angela's heart was full, and I began to understand a little more.

When we got home from the hospital, I expected there to be a lot more lamenting and tears. I expected Angela to need more time. As I mentioned before, I was a little surprised that Angela was so peaceful when her doctor told her she only had a few days. Angela had surrendered her grief. God was making her heart ready, and in her surrender and her willingness to offer her suffering for others, God was faithful and was already showing that faithfulness. The holiness of that room was a testimony to the incredible grace that was being poured out.

As Angela said to Tom Booth, "… everything we do is surrendering to God and His will with joy." There lies the greatest lesson Angela would teach us. She did not want to die at 32. She did not want to leave her children, her husband, her friends, her hopes for our future, her dreams of a long life, but God allowed her to go through this trial, and she was willing to accept whatever came of it. Despite the great pain she would express while coming to terms with her looming death, Angela offered that pain back to God and it became a beautiful offering. That offering, that surrender, that self-sacrifice not only brought her great joy, but it brought many to faith and it brought healing to many. If we offer our whole selves back to God as a pleasing sacrifice, an offering, He will make all things new.

Now a couple weeks after Angela nearly died in my arms, and I told the world that it was almost time to say goodbye, she still had life left in her, and it seemed it was for a purpose greater than any of us could comprehend. She had already surrendered and now she was allowing God's work to be done in her, in our family, in our friends, and in all those who would come to know her story.

At the Hour of Death

A DREAM

"She wants you to escort her in for her last," the nameless man said to me as he led me to an elevator. I did not know who she was or to where I was escorting her. The elevator door opened and I exited. I was wearing a tuxedo, and a few steps in front of me there was a red carpet and an elegantly dressed woman stood waiting. I was led to her side but did not see her face. She took my arm, and we waited to go forward. I now could see that there were many people all around us, and they were cheering. My view changed a bit, and I could see that we were on a roof-top of what seemed to be a tall building. Not only were there people surrounding us on the building, but down below many more thousands also stood cheering. It seemed I was escorting her on stage for some grand performance. I'm not sure if I was told this or intuited it, but it seemed this was an encore or grand finale. The anticipation grew and so did the volume of the crowd. I looked at her and she was ready, so we walked forward; as we got to the top of the ramp, I stopped and she kept going out onto what seemed to be a large round stage that jetted out from the building so that all below could see her. I was filled with eager anticipation and chills ran over my body. Just as she took the microphone and began to sing, the crowd cheered louder and louder, there was a burst of light or fireworks, and I noticed she now had some sort of crown upon her head. I was filled with an incredible sense of joy. At that very moment I woke up, realizing it was all a dream.

This wasn't a dream I could wake up from and fall right back to sleep; I jumped out of bed and was wide awake. The dream seemed so very real, yet I had no clue what it meant. I was, however, filled with joy, and I also noticed it was just about 3 a.m. I had woken up at 3 a.m. most nights while Angela was in hospice care and had realized this was a time for me to pray. I sat by Angela's bed and prayed the 3 O'clock Prayer followed by the Divine Mercy Chaplet. I contemplated the dream some but didn't think a whole lot more of it after that night. It wasn't until after Angela's death that I would make the connection that the woman was Angela, and I was escorting her to heaven. The people all around represented the angels and saints in heaven, the many family and friends who so lovingly were caring for our family, those from our church communities and the thousands of people from around the world who were praying so heavily for Angela and for our family. It was as near a vision of the Communion of Saints praying someone into heaven as I could ever have had. I was escorting Angela to her grand finale, her encore performance, her great journey from this life into the next; all around us were many who had witnessed the heroic surrender and faithfulness of Angela, and they were praying and cheering her on for her great courage

I finally realized the significance of this dream a few days after Angela's actual death while talking over the funeral Mass and

Vigil with Tom Booth who was coming to do music. Something he said reminded me of the dream and so I told him about it. He said, "I hope you're going to tell that story in your eulogy." I did not yet know how to explain the dream, and honestly, I felt as though it may be a little too strange for people. However, as I've continued to reflect on Angela's death and the work God has done in and through it all, I have begun to see even more clearly how this dream was a glimpse of the spiritual reality of what was going on in our lives. As I look at Angela's final days and her actual death, it becomes clearer.

Father Michael Scanlan, former President of Franciscan University of Steubenville shared a poignant story when I was a student which helps me understand this dream and the reality of what happened with Angela. He spoke of a student from the university who was able to meet Blessed Pope John Paul II. He had a Franciscan University of Steubenville shirt on and upon seeing the shirt, Blessed John Paul II said to the young man, "Ah, Steubenville. Coraggio!" Franciscan University and its student body is known for having great courage in living out their faith and proclaiming the truth. The Pontiff was affirming that great courage.

Father Scanlan then told the story of a close family's little boy. It has been many years since I heard this story, but I will give my memorized version. We'll call the boy Billy. Father Scanlan was with the family at a celebration at a community pool. Billy was a young boy around the age of five. At one point while everyone was swimming and having a good time, Billy shyly walked over to the high dive. With great wonder Billy looked up at the diving board and watched for a while as older kids jumped in. Taking an account of what was before him, Billy took a breath and began heading up the steps. As he climbed the steps, his family and friends began to notice, and slowly everyone's eyes were fixed on Billy, now at the top of the high dive. Billy stood at the back of the high dive and seemed to rethink his plan. As Billy's nerves grew, the family and friends gathered round and began to call out to him: "Go for it, Billy!" "You can do it, Billy!" He hesitated longer, and at one point, he began to step back to the ladder as if to come down. Just then the loved ones began to get louder and louder: "Be brave, Billy!" "We know you can do this!" "Go, Billy. Go, Billy. Go, Billy!" Some of the children began to chant. Billy took a big breath and stepped forward. Now everyone was screaming and cheering louder and louder. Billy stepped to the very edge of the diving board and silence fell. With one decisive motion, Billy jumped headlong into the cool water and the family erupted with joy: "Coraggio!" Father Scanlan concluded. The angels and saints are cheering you on. They are shouting, "Coraggio!" Take courage. This story, which I have never forgotten since first hearing it, gave me great perspective about my dream and my understanding of Angela's suffering.

ONE WEEK BEFORE DEATH

"I think I'm just ready to go. I'm tired, and I'm ready for this to be over," Angela said.

I inquired why she was ready, "Was it because of the pain?"

"I just don't know if I see the point of being here anymore; I'm a burden to you and the kids and I'm just so tired." She had been in significant pain and had not been able to eat anything of substance for some time. Angela's feeding tube was no longer use-able because the tumors were pushing in on her stomach so much that all food and drink, whether put into the tube or her mouth, was just being pushed out through the tube site. Most of anything she drank would also drain out the tube site. The leakage was so great that we had to fashion a colostomy bag around the tube site to collect the fluid. Angela was extremely thirsty, however, and so I was draining the bag almost every hour. I asked her if I was mak-ing her feel like a burden.

She said no, but I noticed a hesitation.

I inquired more, "Is it because I have asked you to slow down on drinking fluids so fast because of draining the bag?"

"Yes," she replied.

I realized that while my intent was simply practical – I couldn't drain the bag fast enough some days because I also had to take care of the kids and had many other duties - I was making her feel like a burden. I quickly let her know that she was not a burden and that I would do anything she needed. "Angela, I will give you whatever you need to be comfortable, and you are not a burden! I'm so happy you are still here." I explained to her how this extra time was so good for the kids, for me, and for all of those who loved her. I told her that the point was for us to say goodbye and that while I knew she was ready, God was giving us this time. I also explained to her how the kids were learning profound lessons in watching her go.

She grinned and said, "You really think so?"

"Yes!" I exclaimed. "Yes! Angela, do you remember the day you came out of the shower in tears and you told me, 'I just want the kids to know Jesus, to love Jesus. I want that to be the most important thing.' Do you remember that?"

"Yes, of course."

"Angela, as you lie here and accept what is coming, as you surrender, as you do it with a smile on your face and as you pray, you are changing all of us, and you are teaching me, the kids and many others what it really means for Jesus to be the most important thing." She grinned. Next I said, "I get it. I understand that this is so hard for you, and it is so hard to just lie in bed. But God knows the right time. I trust that He will take you when the time is right. Until then, I know that you are here for a reason and I don't care how many times I have to change your bag or refill your drink or wipe your face. Just having you here is worth it. And Gianna and Augustine - I see the way they cherish each moment as they sit with you in bed or come to check on you. Your being here is helping them accept this." With a smile, she squeezed my hand and fell back to sleep.

Over the next few days she would speak much less as each day passed and sleep much more. Her awake periods were sometimes lucid, but most times, she was incoherent. She would watch as people spoke to her and tried to respond with smiles and nods, but not a whole lot more. Her pain had increased greatly over these next few days. Then on Monday they subsided significantly. During this brief reprieve from the pain, Angela was able to talk a little bit more, though still in broken and incomplete sentences.

Angela's body had continued to decline and more organs showed signs of shutting down. Still, as she lied in bed, her peace and beauty radiated in the room. On Monday we sat together and I read to her and asked her some questions. I asked her at one point, "Do you ever regret our life?"

She responded, "No. I didn't want it to end like this, but it is all making sense to me now. I understand now." She never clarified what she understood, but I think Angela was beginning to understand the purpose of not only the suffering of cancer but of all the suffering in her life. Though she couldn't explain what she understood, there was clarity in her words and now I could comprehend the peace she had.

TILL DEATH DO US PART

I sat with Angela as much as I could, holding her hand, playing music and praying many prayers, yet I would find myself feeling very restless and anxious. There is no more helpless feeling than sitting by a loved one's side waiting for them to die. I felt as if I should be doing something. To move away from the instincts of trying to help her live, of doing everything I could to fight this disease, towards suddenly giving up was painful and heart wrenching. I had discerned our decision to move Angela home with hospice care with the help of very knowledgeable friends who walked me through the process of making this decision. It was clear that Angela's body was in the pre-active dying process, and that there really was nothing we could do to stop it. One friend posed the decision this way: "At some point it is time to surrender to God and if she is in the pre-active dying process, it might be that time to accept death."

I was confident that we had made the right choice, but as I sat in her room, I felt helpless and useless. I would rethink my decisions and question myself. "Am I giving up too soon?" This wasn't helped, of course, by a few well-meaning people who voiced that they thought I was giving up hope. So in my restlessness and uneasiness I would pace, find things to do and find myself getting frustrated. As I would come back into the room, I would look at Angela's peaceful face, and I would realize that my only job was to just be present to her and to wait patiently with her for death. When I finally surrendered to this reality, that my only job was to just be present to her, I felt an incredible peace.

One particular afternoon, just a few days before she died, I sat with Angela and held her hand as I read to her. She would occasionally look up and listen or smile. I would tell her how much I loved and cherished her and she would respond with a faint response. At one point she whispered, "I always knew you would cherish me to the end." As she fell back to sleep, I looked down at our hands and her ring was missing. It had fallen off several times, as Angela was so frail that it was now too large for her finger. She had placed it on the table next to her bed. I picked up the ring and placed it on her finger and held her hand again. I gazed upon our hands, reflecting on that ring and what it symbolized, on our hands and the symbolism of husband and wife walking hand in hand through life. I thought about the first time we held hands. It was on our first date to Cirque du Soleil. At one point Angela had moved her hand near mine and then gently touched my hand. I took her hand till the crowd erupted in applause and a standing ovation. Angela never admitted to holding my hand that night. She would say, "I did not hold your hand that night. I wasn't ready." I would laugh and remind her of the many things she did during that time of friendship – when she supposedly did not want to date yet - like lean on me, touch my hand, and even press her cheek against mine for a long time, as if to wait for a kiss. She would laugh at me and say, "Whatever, I was not that forward." I then thought about when we did finally hold hands after we were "officially" dating. There is something remarkable about holding hands when you are falling in love.

Many people say it's in the kiss that you know, or it's love at first sight; I tend to think it's in the hands. Holding hands was not always romantic, but holding hands was our constant connection to one another. Even when in an argument or a difficult conversation, we would often hold hands. When Angela was struggling with depression, I held her hands many times just to calm her, to soothe her, to help her feel supported. Angela, too, would hold my hand when I was having a hard day or down about my job situation or our financial hurdles. A simple touch of her hand would instantly soothe me.

Through Angela's cancer journey, holding hands had become our primary form of intimacy. Whether Angela was receiving chemotherapy, waiting for surgery or simply resting at home, we would spend lots of time holding hands, talking, praying and simply being present. As I held her hand during this seventeen-month journey, I would often squeeze and hold her hand very tightly as I thought about losing her, as if I could somehow hold her tight enough to keep her from dying. Now sitting in our room as she lie in wait for death, holding her hand was literally all I had left. She could hardly speak or even acknowledge my words; I simply had to hold her hand to communicate my love and to be sure she knew she was not alone. Indeed, I would be there till the end.

As I thought about her hands, I also thought about that ring, the one I gave her as I asked her to be my bride and the ring that stood as a symbol of this life-long Sacrament of Marriage. With that ring came our promise to love one another fully and completely until death came for one of us. The wedding ring speaks of permanence, of commitment, of an unbreakable bond between a husband and wife. Yet that ring could not bind her any longer; it could not keep her from dying, and it certainly could not keep her from heaven.

As I sat in this moment, I wanted to capture our hands one last time. I took a picture that I later shared. It is the image of us holding hands with Angela's ring as the focal point of the image. A week or so earlier I had verbally told Angela that she was free to go home. My words on that day were, "You took my hand and you have loved me well. When Jesus comes and offers you his hand, you are free to go." After taking the picture of our hands I felt I should say those words again. So I wrote them down and then read them to Angela:

"Till Death"
As if I could keep you longer, I placed this ring back on your finger today. It had fallen off a few times.

Oh, that this ring could keep you here longer. It is a mark of our commitment; it is my promise to love you with my whole heart, and yet there is a love greater than mine that will take you soon. How could this mere piece of gold compare to the love of God, which loves you completely, wholly, and perfectly?

It cannot, so I will hold your hand a little while longer. I will keep putting this ring back on your finger. But when the

*time comes and He asks you for your hand, you are free to
go. Go to that perfect love which makes all things new. Go
and be whole again. For now, till death do we part.*

Though nothing truly prepares you to say goodbye to
your spouse, I thought back upon an experience that I could see
in hindsight was meant to prepare me for this difficult goodbye.
It was around the time Angela and I were engaged. I remember
waking up one morning and thinking about Angela, about our
love, about our dreams for our life together. It was at first an overwhelming feeling of love. Then, in an instant, I recall having this
realization that she was not mine forever, that one day she would
leave or I would leave, and one of us would be left behind. I recall
very clearly feeling a sinking in my gut for several days. It was
almost a grief. Little did I know that I would actually experience
letting Angela go so soon.

This seemed a morbid thought for such an exciting time,
as we prepared for marriage, so I tried to move away from this feeling, to let it go. I talked with Angela and a few friends about it, and
I prayed. Yet the sinking feeling didn't leave me at once. I simply
had to feel that heartache for a couple of weeks. Eventually the
feeling left me, but not before I gained some very valuable insight.
Sometime later, I wrote a letter to a young friend named Daniel
who was about to be married that will better express what I understood through this experience:

*It can seem quaint to say, "We are called to lead each other
to heaven," but when you fully understand that your love
will not outlast her existence, that one day she will go to a*

love that will swallow your love whole, that at some point she will drink from a fountain of love so great and so vast that the love you gave her will barely seem like a drop of water on the tongue in comparison, it is then that you can understand that this is not a quaint thought. This is an awesome and supernatural responsibility. Because if you fail to get her to heaven, then you know where she will go – that place where she will never taste love again.

I tell you with great confidence that having this knowledge early on was an absolute grace, not only because I would have to face that reality so much sooner than I would have ever thought or hoped, but also because in having that understanding, I was able to more fully understand the purpose of my role in her life. So here, as I sat in this reality of letting go of Angela, I was able to say and pen the words above. God had prepared my heart for such a time as this; He had placed this understanding deep within so that when the time came to let Angela go, I would remember that my love could not outlast her existence and that a greater love was waiting to take her home.

THE THIN VEIL

As I shared in the previous chapter, Angela had clearly begun to experience some profound encounters with heaven and it was becoming clear that there was a "thin veil" between heaven and earth. Many who came to see Angela would remark that it was almost as if she had one foot in heaven and one on earth. As she drew nearer to death, the veil only grew more and more thin. It seemed Angela was halfway to heaven already, yet her journey was not complete. While she felt at peace and ready to go, and while she was tiring of this fading life and the pain and suffering she was enduring, her journey continued. Father Parks came to see Angela again and to give her what is known by many as "last rites." Father Parks had seen Angela only two weeks earlier, but given Angela's worsening pain and decline, I felt that it was important that Angela have this once again. Father Parks sat by Angela's side and just as with other important visits during this time, Angela was more awake than she had been most of that day. The last rites are meant to prepare a person's soul for death. It includes three Sacraments: Anointing of the Sick, in which the priest prays for healing and relief of suffering; Penance, in which we receive forgiveness of sins; and the Eucharist, which when given to the dying is known as viaticum. Father Parks shared with Angela that he was going to give her communion. As Catholics, we believe that the Eucharist, also referred to as communion, is the body and blood of Christ made present through the prayers of Consecration during the Mass. For us it is a time when, as some theologians would say, "heaven kisses earth." While Father Parks had brought Angela Eucharist before, he shared something special with Angela on this visit; though communion is something Catholics receive regularly, it has a special purpose at the end of one's life. Referred to as viaticum, the Eucharist given to the dying is literally meant to be strength for the journey. Father Parks shared this with Angela and explained what that word meant. Viaticum, he shared, means literally "provision for the journey." He told her that when a servant was sent on a long journey, the master would give them provisions, be it food, supplies or other resources, which they would need to be safe and to be strengthened and nourished on their trek. The Eucharist, he told her, would give her the grace and strength to make this journey to heaven. It was a beautiful moment as Angela took that small piece of the host in her mouth and smiled as she tried to swallow it down. I don't recall what Angela said to Father Parks, but knowing her love of God and especially her love of the Eucharist, I knew in her smile that these words and this grace were comforting and brought her peace. I later found the story of St. Elizabeth Ann Seton, who upon receiving the Eucharist on her deathbed exclaimed, "One communion more, and then eternity."

During this last week we began to see Angela staring off into corners of the room and at times, seeming to have conversations with someone. There were times I would walk in the room, and it was as if I had interrupted a conversation. I didn't know who she was looking at or talking to, but since she had told me she was talking to saints and angels, I simply assumed she was entertaining heaven. The kids began to notice this as well and would sit and watch her face. "I think Mommy's talking to an angel, Daddy," they would say. They would lovingly stand by her side and hold her hand as I said prayers, and they would lean over to give her kisses a couple of times a day.

About two days before Angela died, Gianna and Augustine had noticed she was seeing angels more and more. They would watch her on the video monitor downstairs and would see her looking all over the room as if she was seeing many things. They then saw many piercing lights cutting across the screen. I came to see what they saw; it was as if there were prisms in the room that were shooting rays of light at all different angles. What was most incredible was that these piercing lights even cut through the rays of light coming through our bedroom window.

That day I had come to Angela's side to ask her if we could pray for all of the people who were praying for us and those who had been sending in prayer requests. A two weeks earlier, when people started telling me they were experiencing healing of their own, I had begun sharing on our Facebook page that people could send in their prayer requests, and Angela and I would pray for them. Many, many people wrote in with their needs and Angela offered her sufferings for those requests during our prayer time. I thought perhaps that Angela could die that day, given her decline, and I felt an urging that it was time to pray for these intentions one last time. When I entered the room, she was staring up and had a glow about her face; she tried to talk to me but couldn't get out the words. I can best describe this experience by sharing what I shared that day on Facebook:

Today as I sat by Angela's side, I asked her if I could pray with her. She had been trying to say something previously but couldn't. When I asked her, she struggled to say, "It's too hard to talk because of the angel." I said it's ok. I'd say the prayer and she could just rest. I asked again, "Are you seeing an angel?" She said, "Yes." The whole time I prayed she was looking around the room. Her face, which had been very ashen and dry, was its normal beautiful color and seemed to glisten.

I prayed a Chaplet of Divine Mercy and explained that I wanted to offer our prayers for all of you and for your requests. I had also just asked her again to offer her suffer-ings today for all of you. So we prayed. She did mouth some

*of the prayers at times, but mostly just looked around the
room. I prayed four decades for all of you and offered the
last decade for Angela's healing.*

*Know that she is very aware that she is praying for all of you
and smiles when I ask her to take your needs to the throne
when she goes to heaven.*

The power of this moment and this day was truly something out
of this world. I let her sleep and left the room. An hour or so later I
returned to Angela's side and sat at her feet praying. It was around
3 p.m., so I imagine I would have been praying the Divine Mercy
Chaplet. As I sat and watched Angela and she looked around the
room, I noticed that she was now very actively looking up and her
eyes widened. I asked Gianna and Augustine to come up stairs
and they sat on the bed and watched her. "What's happening?"
Gianna asked. "I think she is seeing an angel or maybe God,"
I told her. Her face was even brighter and full of color, and her
eyes widened as big as I had ever seen. There was an intense look
of wonder on her face and her mouth opened with a wide smile.
She sat up a little, and I truly thought that perhaps this was the
moment she would die. As she gazed into something that you and I
likely have never seen, I thought this would be the perfect moment
to die. Gianna and Augustine were just as amazed as I was while
they watched. "Isn't this amazing that Mommy is seeing angels?"
I asked. "Yes!" They exclaimed in unison. I sat thanking God for
giving us this moment, this chance to see into this encounter with
heaven. After a while, Angela's face relaxed and she looked around
the room and followed Gianna, Augustine, and me with her eyes.

AT THE HOUR OF DEATH

She fell back to sleep and the kids left the room.

ANGELA'S LAST GREAT SUFFERING

After this heavenly encounter, I thought that perhaps Angela would pass in the night. She never fully regained consciousness after that afternoon encounter. Instead, she entered into an intense period of suffering that evening that continued for about thirty-six hours. Angela had suffered from terminal restlessness throughout these last few weeks but with proper medication, I was able to help keep it under control. This last thirty-six hours, however, the medication didn't seem to be working. It also seemed that she was in severe pain and discomfort. Many times her episodes intensified, and it seemed as if she was in some sort of struggle or fight. I spoke with Angela's nurses and her doctor several times; we changed up protocols and tried many things, but nothing seemed to help.

The next day I began to wonder if something else was at hand. I called her doctor one last time and expressed how much more intense this restlessness and agitation had become and that none of the recommendations were working. Finally she said, "Chris, it sounds to me that this may be something spiritual and not medical. Would you be able to get someone to come see her, or do you want the chaplain from hospice to come?" I told her that I had been thinking the same thing and after some more conversation and encouragement, I hung up and immediately called Father Parks.

Father Parks returned my call, and I explained to him what was going on. He immediately came to the house and sat with

Angela. Again he anointed her and administered the Sacraments. As he finished I said to him, "Father, I think this is more than "terminal restlessness." I'm starting to think that maybe she is undergoing some last great suffering or some final struggle. What do you think?" We sat in silent prayer together for some time, and then he looked to me and said, "I think you are right. Can we pray some more?" He then opened up to a body of prayers that he said he had never really prayed. They were a series of prayers called "Commendations for the Dying." We prayed several of the prayers together and interceded heavily for Angela in this suffering. Her suffering didn't end immediately, but she did calm quite a bit. Father Parks left and I sat by her side most of that night. A few family members came to pray as well and sat in the room silently praying the rosary for Angela. They shared that during the prayers Angela calmed but then began the restlessness again after they finished.

The intense prayer continued between me and other family throughout the night. I asked many to pray for her during these difficult hours and shared only with those closest that I thought this was some great suffering she was enduring. That night, after putting the children down to bed, I sat by Angela's side praying heavily. Slowly her restlessness got less intense. At about midnight I decided to lie down with the kids and try to get some sleep. It was difficult to allow myself to sleep while she struggled, but just as I got into bed, she calmed significantly and I fell asleep. I woke an hour or so later and checked on her. She was now calm and resting well, so I went back to sleep

At 3 a.m. I woke up and immediately could hear that Angela's breathing had changed. I went to her side. She was peace-

AT THE HOUR OF DEATH

fully resting and her breathing had changed significantly. They
tell you that a dying person's breathing will change shortly before
death, but no one can adequately describe what that change is like.
I knew right away that she had entered her final hours. The breathing is almost like a series of sighs one after another. I checked for
a pulse and her pulses in her wrists were gone. I had been told that
once her pulses disappeared, she would likely have about three to
six hours left.

THE HOUR OF DEATH

Knowing Angela had only a few hours to live, I pulled a
chair to her bedside, held her hand and began to pray the Divine
Mercy Chaplet. I sat with her for several hours praying, talking to
her, telling her of my love and encouraging her to make the journey to heaven in peace. All the while I held her hand. As I would
speak to her, she would occasionally squeeze my hand. I sat there
by her side for five hours, praying, crying, and saying goodbye.
Our children were in the room lying in our bed and fast asleep.
I wondered if I should wake them to say goodbye. Instead, I just
prayed that God would allow them to wake up before she passed if
it was His Will.

Around 7:30 a.m. Angela's respirations had decreased and
she no longer squeezed my hand. She was still there, but it seemed
she was no longer in my hands. There was a marked change and I
felt it would be a matter of minutes. I sat watching the kids, hoping
they would wake up. Around 8 a.m. both Gianna and Augustine
began to stir, and one-by-one, they woke up and came to my side. I
held them in my lap as I explained to them that Mommy was about

to die. They both looked at her, but neither said anything. They simply buried their heads in my neck. I asked them if they wanted to say goodbye. They both declined. After some time, Augustine asked to go downstairs. I said we would go down for a minute to grab something to eat, but we had to come back up. As we left the room I stopped and said to Gianna, "Are you sure you don't want to say goodbye to Mommy? Are you sure you don't want to kiss her one last time?"

She replied, "I want to kiss her, but I don't want to say goodbye."

"Ok," I said, and I took them back in the room. I lifted Gianna to Angela, and she kissed her on the head. As I pulled her back to me, Angela let out one final breath. It was 8:16 a.m. on September 21, 2012.

It was finished. As quickly as her breath left her, it was over. I felt her chest and it was hard as a rock and her skin cold to the touch. Her body, though it looked exactly as it did only seconds before, was so cold, so dead, so empty. We stood over her lifeless body, Augustine in my right arm, Gianna in my left, and we prayed. I told the children she was gone, and they each looked back at her and then put their heads back down on my shoulder. They didn't cry or say anything. They just sat in the silence.

While Angela's body lay there lifeless, absent of her soul, it would be easy to say that this was the end of this story, that there is nothing more to tell. It would be easy for me to finish this chapter by simply saying, "It is finished," or "The end." Yet we know in faith that there is so much more that we didn't see as Angela left this life and went onto the next. Instead, I will close our story with a letter that I've written to my children.

What We Didn't See

Dear Gianna and Augustine,

It was September 21, 2012 when your mother died. You both remember all too well how much pain and suffering she had been through. You were there when she died and I believe she waited for you both to wake up before she went to heaven. I think she wanted you to see her one last time before she took her last breath. She took her last breath just as Gianna gave her one last kiss.

In this book I have told the story of your mother because I promised her I would, so that others would know that they must trust in Jesus no matter what. That's what she asked for. I also wrote this story for the two of you; so that you would always know the great faith your mother had and would be able to look back on how she changed so many lives. I've told lots of stories and details here about the things that happened before your mother died and even how she died. But there are so many things I can't fully tell because when your mother left this life, she went to a place we cannot go. I can tell you all about her life, her cancer, her pain, her faith, her joy and even her death, but there is so much more that we didn't see.

What we didn't see is that while Mommy was lying in that bed waiting to die and holding my hand, Jesus was there, too. She had a dream she shared with Father Parks that when she died I was there holding her tight and comforting her in her pain and then suddenly I was replaced, and it was Jesus holding her and she had no more pain and she was home in heaven. We didn't get to see Jesus hold her, but I believe in my heart that it is true.

We didn't see the angels come down from heaven to take Mommy's soul. We didn't see the angels and saints in heaven waiting to welcome her home. We didn't see them erupt in great cheers as they welcomed her with great joy, just like we didn't see all of the thousands of people on earth who were praying for Mommy to make her way to heaven. But we know they were.

Gianna, do you remember how St. Gianna's daughter, Gianna Emanuela promised to pray for Mommy and to pray that her mother would welcome Mommy into heaven? We didn't get to see St. Gianna welcome her, but I'm certain that she did.

We didn't see how God healed many people who were praying for Mommy and how many people grew in their faith by watching your mother continue to trust in God. We couldn't see what God was doing in other people's hearts, but we know that He changed many lives.

We didn't get to see Mommy's great big smile as she saw heaven and as she made her way there. We didn't get to see her incredible joy as she got to see the Father, Son and the Holy Spirit for the very first time. We don't get to see what Mommy's life is like in heaven now, but I am certain it is all joy.

We don't get to see Mommy praying alongside the Virgin Mary, or St. Augustine, St. Faustina, or Blessed John

Paul II, and we can't see her sitting beside her favorite, St. Therese, but don't you believe that she is there by her side?

What you saw was your mother get sick, suffer a lot, and try her hardest to get better, but she didn't. What you saw were a lot of hard times and what you saw was that Mommy left this earth, but what I hope you'll always remember is that even though Mommy was sick and suffering and never got better, she always trusted Jesus. She still found her joy in God and she believed in the promise of heaven more than anything. She wanted to get better, but she trusted that if God wouldn't heal her, He knew what was best. She trusted that if she had to go, God would take care of both of you and that our family would be alright. Mommy knew that even if God didn't heal her, He would make the best of this hard situation for us because she believed He wanted what was best for us always.

What you didn't see was that all the while Mommy was suffering, she was praying for you, Gianna and you, Augustine, that you would always know God and trust in Him. She didn't want to die so soon, but she wanted to be sure you knew that no matter what, you must trust in Jesus. She told me once before she died, that the only thing she cared about with you two was that you would always know that having a relationship with Jesus was the most important thing.

There are a lot of things we didn't see. We didn't get to see the saints and angels Mommy saw before she died, but we did see the incredible joy in Mommy's face when she saw them. What we didn't see doesn't matter because of what we know in our hearts: Mommy had great faith in God and in

His promise; Mommy trusted in God and she wants us to trust in Him with everything we have.

The story of Mommy's life would be incomplete if we only looked at the things we could see. The real story of Mommy's life is the story of how God used her pain, her sickness, her suffering and her great faith to change many people's lives. I know because she changed mine. Ultimately, the complete story of Mommy's life is that her life here on earth was only the beginning. Her life goes on in heaven for eternity. The real story is that your mother is only gone from this earth; in heaven she is full of life and full of joy, and she is praying for you and me every day. She is there with God and she is where she always wanted to be. That's the real story: Mommy is in the one place she wanted more than anything, and she's waiting for us to one day join her there along with the whole Communion of Saints.

Gianna, Augustine – I pray you will never forget to trust in Jesus, no matter what. I pray you will trust in God's divine plan completely and that you will always remember that it's not what you see that matters; what really matters is that you grow in faith, hope and love and always surrender your life to God with great JOY. If you do this, then one day you both will be in heaven too, with Mommy and all those angels and saints experiencing incredible joy.

With great love,
Daddy

Life on this earth and our ultimate death are but a prelude; they are the opening score. On the other side of that curtain, lies a promise that is greater than anything you or I can ever dream of on this earth.

~~The End.~~

The Beginning...

Afterword

ON THE MORNING YOU WENT HOME

Death had come and gone. Though her body lay lifeless in our room, Angela was gone from this place. Gone, to meet her Maker, presumably to experience the ecstasy of heaven and the joy of the communion of saints. This side of heaven, the thin veil that we experienced while she was dying, was now like an iron curtain, an impenetrable barrier between her and us.

Angela's sojourn on this earth was over, but for Gianna, Augustine, and I, along with all of Angela's family and friends, our sojourn had all but just begun. Angela breathed her last that Friday morning and with each hour, each meal, each bedtime, each waking, we faced this new life without the woman we all loved so dearly. While her last breath only lasted but a second – a sigh so final and so different from all her other breaths – that day lasted a lifetime. Many phone calls, many conversations, and many decisions followed.

We took our time letting her go, and asked the mortuary to wait a few hours to take her lifeless body away. This gave family and close friends time to say a final goodbye. Our children

IT IS WELL - LIFE IN THE STORM

circled about the house but did not seem to fully understand. They came one last time into the bedroom as I explained to them that Mommy's body would be taken away. They were slightly confused still, not quite sure if she was gone, as they could still see her lying there. We spent a few moments saying goodbye and then they left with family and friends who took them across the way to our favorite neighborhood restaurant to eat. The house was silent, with only a few of our family staying to support me as the mortuary transport arrived. I had been told that morning to be "present to the moment" as her body was taken away. I gathered my father and stepmother into the bedroom to say some final prayers over Angela's body. Then I watched in silent vigil as the men carried her down the stairs, laid her on the gurney, and put her in the van. I stood there in the drive as they drove away and I let reality take hold.

A short while later I joined my children and family for lunch. There was a brief relief in the finality of it all, but still a sinking feeling in my gut. That sinking feeling was masked by the practical tasks at hand. My children were being well distracted by our family and that allowed me to be well distracted by all of my duties in honoring my now late wife.

As the day came to a close, I got the children ready for bed. They had been sleeping with Angela and me these last few months and so I brought them into the master bedroom. Once they were ready for bed, I asked them to hop into bed and we would pray. Only my son didn't jump right into bed. He sat on the floor of our bedroom. Again I called him to bed and he didn't come.

"Son, why are you sitting there?"

He quietly replied, "This is a special place." He was sitting in the very spot that Angela's hospice bed had been for the last five weeks. There he sat in the place she breathed her last. He repeated himself as if to emphasize what he had said, "This is a special place."

Holding back the rush of tears, I said, "Oh, Augustine, do you think we should sit there for our prayer time?"

He nodded his head yes and I immediately came to sit by him. Gianna jumped out of bed to join us. We sat in a circle and I led us in prayer. We talked for a few minutes about how we felt and each shared something we would miss about Angela. We all cried. We ended with a fun memory and got back into bed. As we talked and prayed, I held back the tears as best I could. Once they were asleep, a fountain of tears came with a feeling of heaviness, like a brick on my chest.

Augustine was one day shy of three years old and yet he knew all too well the gravity of it all... I think in a sense he wanted to savor this final day with his mother. It was the last day he would ever wake to her alive. He would wake on his third birthday without. Everyday following, he and Gianna and I would wake one day further from her being in our lives. Waking up without is a feeling like no other. Anyone who has lost a loved one knows this heartache.

There is a book Angela loved to read to the kids called *On the Night You Were Born*, by Nancy Tillman. It starts out with a beautiful prose about the wonderful night of the child's birth:

*On the night you were born, the moon smiled with such
wonder that the stars peeked in to see you and the night*

wind whispered, "Life will never be the same." Because there had never been anyone like you... ever in the world.

The book goes on to speak of all creation being enchanted with this new child and it ends with this powerful line:

For never before in story or rhyme (not even once upon a time) has the world ever known a you, my friend, and it never will, not ever again...

I think often of this story, which comes from the heart of a mother to her child. I think of the other side of that coin, when life comes to an end and how the words turn to express something entirely different. Perhaps my rewriting of this quote will help to illustrate my heart on that night:

On the morning you went home it was as if the sadness darkened the sun, and as we peered in to see you, there was no life to be found and the breeze on this first day of fall seemed to whisper, "She has already gone away." Life will never be the same. Because there had never been anyone like you... ever in the world... For never before in story or rhyme has the world ever known a you, my friend, and it never will, not ever again.

Death had come and death had gone and with it Angela went away. Yet death did not take Angela far, only to the other side, to the end of this life. Death has no hold on those who love and serve our Lord. Yet, the other side can seem so far away when the iron curtain between heaven and earth drops to the ground.

While sadness reigned in our home, there was a persistent joy that permeated even the saddest of days. There is no enjoyment in planning the funeral of your young bride, save perhaps the sense of pride in planning to honor her in a way that is befitting of her incredible life. Death had come and we were left in its wake. Even though Angela's absence was painful, death could not take her far and death could not take from us that which mattered most. That is our faith, our hope in the resurrection, and that persistent joy. There was darkness as we sat on the floor at Augustine's request, but there was also a joy that came from that short time of prayer and reminiscing. A joy came out of each of my children, a joy that can only come from something greater than our human frailty.

TELL HIM IT'S ALL JOY

It was three days after the last time I held her hand, the time she breathed her last. I sat on my sofa ready to read the day's emails and messages. I received lots of messages every day from people I knew and people I didn't know. Most of them were condolences, but many of them also came with beautiful messages of hope. In those days following Angela's death, I received countless messages telling me how Angela had in one way or another impacted people's lives. As I read through the messages, one came from a former co-worker who had followed our sojourn and shared our story with those he knew. Dan was passing along a message from one of his friends who had been praying for Angela. We did not know this woman personally, but she had come to know us through praying for us. She wrote:

I was at Mass last evening. Right after Communion, I was praying with my eyes closed – I felt rather infused with light and heard this very beautiful laughter - very contagious, tinkling, joyous laughter - and a woman's voice said, "It's all joy - tell him it's all joy." I don't know why, but I feel like it was Angela Faddis. Please remember, I've never met this family, never encountered them at all before you very graciously shared their site. I wasn't even sure I was going to pass this on until I read her obituary this morning - the word joy kept popping out and I read about her infectious laugh - and that was the sound of this laugh that I heard.
- Kathy

I recall being filled with peace and joy upon reading this. There was a clear sense that this experience was authentic and meant to be shared with me. As we neared the funeral, these words rang in my head. I knew they were true in my heart of hearts. Just to be sure I knew, God confirmed them through several other stories I would hear and messages I would receive over the next several months. Another woman wrote me a month after Angela's death to say:

I had a dream and your beautiful wife was in it. I was dreaming about being somewhere and there were a lot of people outside maybe a mall or something... Everyone looked up to the sky, and we saw someone coming down from the clouds, it was the Virgin Mary, she appeared and perhaps spoke (but I don't remember), then three other women were with her... they each came forward and said their names and each said some words. The last one to come forward was your wife. She had a huge smile and was laugh-

*ing. She said her name and also some words, but I don't
remember exactly what she said. What I do remember was
that joy was definitely one word I heard. – Maribeth*

More stories and messages like these came from people
all around, most of whom we did not know personally. Most of
these folks had never met one another. There were a few consistent
things about each story of a dream or prayer experience involving
Angela. In each account she either said something about joy or
exhibited joy. She often was laughing and smiling brightly in each
account, she was with the Virgin Mary in a few of these experiences, and each person was left feeling joyful and even laughing.
In many of these dreams people could not remember what words
Angela said, other than the word joy, and they remember the
laughter and the smile.

In addition to these stories of encounters with Angela –
either through dreams or during prayer – there is another consistent theme that has come out of the many messages I continue to
get. Many, many folks have shared with me experiences where they
asked Angela to pray for them from heaven to help them in a difficult situation, or to intercede with a miracle for some circumstance
that was causing them great anxiety or depression. Now, I am not
in the business of confirming miracles, but I am amazed at the
amount of people who feel that Angela's intercession was, in their
own words, "powerful." Some have claimed that through her intercession they experienced a miracle, in one way or another. What I
have found most incredible is how many people have shared that
after asking Angela to pray for them, they experienced some sense
of profound or "overwhelming" joy, and many have said that their

anxiety lifted.

"It's all joy, tell him it's all joy." These words and the accounts of others were like salve to my broken heart. They were a reminder of God's faithfulness and a testament to the words of St. James, "Consider it all joy brothers, when you face various trials," (James 1:2). That quote can be quite a paradox when one is dealing with suffering and pain. For many the words of St. James are hard to swallow. "How can I ever consider the dying of my spouse to be something joyful?" I recall one widow telling me in an email. "I refuse to have joy about my husband's death."

I agree. It can seem so out of place to find joy in death. It helps to understand that what St. James is speaking of here is not cheerfulness or gleefulness, nor is he speaking of a happy feeling. Joy here is much deeper than an outward action. Joy, in this sense, is something that resides deep in the soul. This kind of joy comes in knowing that, "All things work for good, for those who love God," (Romans 8:28). This kind of joy permeates the sadness and gives comfort in these times. Sadness and joy can co-exist. This, perhaps, is one of the greatest gifts of Christianity, to have this deep sense of knowing God will indeed win in the end, and our mourning will turn to dancing.

CONSTANT GIFT

About a month or two after Angela's death, I had my own experience in prayer. I was at Mass and having a beautiful time of prayer. Both of the kids were actually praying hard and really paying attention. I felt like this was such grace for me that I could fully enter into prayer during the consecration. I tried to focus on communion with the saints and in particular, imagine Angela being there. I had talked with the kids about this before Mass. We have a mural behind the altar that depicts the communion of saints around the tabernacle and I had explained to them they could look at that mural and imagine Mommy being there.

As we were preparing to receive Communion, I felt like I could see in my mind's eye this joyful image of Angela wearing a dark blue dress, waiting so patiently and joyfully to receive. Now let me be clear, this was not a vision, but my own visualization of this moment. She had her hands folded in front of her face and her eyes were closed. I felt very comforted by this image of her going forward to receive at the true heavenly banquet and then I heard her say to me, "No, I'm not waiting to receive. It is all gift. I am constantly receiving." It was clear to me that the words came from Angela.

In that instant I had a clear understanding that "constantly receiving" meant that the gift of the Eucharist is constantly passing through her and there is no time in which she is not receiving. As we ask the Saints to intercede on our behalf, the grace poured out in the form of miracles or answered prayers is simply the bi-product of the grace that is constantly being poured out to them at the heavenly banquet. As we join ourselves to them in prayer, we simply receive showers of that grace, which is constantly flowing through them. We are receiving the overflow.

It was so strong a gift. After Communion I knelt and simply held that image and those words in my heart. I didn't realize till I got up that tears were streaming down my face. I went through the rest of that day feeling such confident peace.

WE CHOSE JOY

As the days went on without Angela, Gianna and Augustine would go through various emotions and levels of grief. Gianna did not seem to be as sad as one would think she should be. We would often talk about how we were feeling and she said to me on more than one occasion, "I'm not sad for Mommy. She's in heaven, and that's where she should be." Her decision was to be joyful because she knew her mom wanted to be in heaven and she knew in her heart that heaven was our aim. In fact, many months later she would say, "Dad, sometimes I think this world is just a vacation, and heaven is our true home." Gianna's grief came out in little ways here and there, but in general she didn't seem to have the ache that one would expect, at least not early on. (Gianna did eventually face the heartache, though for her that came much later - about two years after Angela's death.)

Augustine experienced much more of the sting of grief early on than did Gianna. He, too, believed whole-heartedly that his mother was in heaven. He, too, would talk about joy, but he seemed to feel the heartache much more. He would often say, "Dad, I just want Mommy to come back." He would sit and bury himself in my arms and cry. Yet, as we would talk and pray, he would always end with a joyful glow of knowing his mother was in heaven.

In many ways Augustine's grief reminded me of how Angela handled her cancer journey. She would often lament and be sad about her fate, but she would always end by turning to her hope in Christ. It was, I think, what most inspired people. Now, here was my three-year-old son exhibiting this same incredible ability to turn mourning into dancing. Here was my daughter, merely five years old, who had the wisdom to understand that while she missed her mother, she was in heaven, and this was something to be happy about.

So what was I to do? I had felt as though I needed to take time off for several months and be present to my children. However, the kids seemed ready to move forward. Gianna asked about going to school and seemed ready to get life started. I was also feeling this urge and push to begin the work God had set on my heart. I'll share more about that work later, but part of that work was completing this very book. Yet it seemed too soon to begin again.

For the most part I had visited many of the stages of grief during Angela's cancer journey. It was probably one of the greatest gifts Angela gave me, to be honest about her grief, and to allow me to do so as well. We grieved her death before she was gone, and we did so together. As such, I believe, I was spared some of the immobilizing heartache that so many experience. However, I would still at times get an overwhelming ache. I recall thinking, "I just don't want to do anything. It hurts too much." In fact, I remember quite clearly one morning that I felt this overwhelming heartache. I went to my bed and lay facing away from the door and I cried. I thought for a moment how I should stay home that day, not get out of bed. I was feeling very sorry for myself in this particular moment. As I cried, I heard footsteps shuffling down the hall. I held back the tears for a moment and the kids came in and shouted in unison, "Dad, can we go do something fun?" They were so excited to get about life. I said yes, and asked them to give me a minute. I lay there a minute longer and I thought, they are ready to begin life again. I also felt as though I could hear Angela saying to me, "You get to wake up to them every day. You get to be the one to experience their lives. Now go."

I got up, I wiped my eyes, and we went out to do something fun. I also set out that day to begin again. Around that time the kids and I talked a lot about joy. I shared with them some of the stories I shared with you about Angela's joy in heaven. We decided as a family that we would choose joy.

Choosing joy didn't mean we didn't grieve. We all still had feelings of sadness. We all still had moments of pain. Yet we decided that each day we would wake up and choose to find joy in the little things. We chose to make the best of this new chapter in our lives. We chose joy by choosing to have hope. We chose joy by choosing to not wallow in our pain, but to live each day in the way Angela lived those last days of her life, with faith and trust. In a practical way, we chose joy by adding something to our nightly prayer. Every night we each shared something we were grateful for to God. This is a practice we continue to this day.

NOW WE BEGIN

"Say with courage: Nunc Coepi – Now I begin, and walk always in the service of God. Do not keep stopping to look back, because he who looks back cannot hasten forward."
Venerable Bruno Lanteri

This phrase, Nunc Coepi – Now I Begin, speaks so adequately to the feeling I had after Angela died. I recall feeling this incredible sense of purpose after she died, as if my work had just begun. Now having decided to choose joy, and to get about our new lives, I had this incredible sense that not only was it time to get our practical lives started, it was time to begin doing the work God had put on my heart. Blessed (soon to be Saint) Theresa of Calcutta said it well, "Yesterday is gone. Tomorrow has yet come. We have only today. Let us begin." So, I began.

I began to figure out what this new life would be. I contacted the school and got Gianna registered to begin kindergarten. I began to make a plan for what I was to do. I set a plan for finishing and publishing this book, began working on the projects that God had put in front of me, and discerned what this next chapter of my career would be.

The kids and I talked a lot about life and moving on. Of the many things we discussed, one topic they brought up often was the possibility of having a "new mom" as they referred to it. I actually was quite shocked that they brought this up so early, as in the first few days after Angela died. I was certainly not really ready for this conversation. I initially just kind of appeased them, "Well I'll take that to prayer, but let's just not worry about that right now." Yet each week it would come up again. Augustine, I felt, was simply hoping to fill this void in his young life. He knew the love of a mother was special and he wanted that love. Gianna, too, wanted that love, but she also had wanted more siblings. One of the things she was most sad about when she learned that Angela would die soon was that she would not get to have another baby brother or sister. She actually talked to me about it the day after we told them that Angela would die.

As they continued to bring it up, I continually told them I'd pray about it. At first I did not really pray about it. I had been of the mindset at one point in my life that you get married once and that's it. I actually had a conversation with Angela when we were engaged. I told her that I didn't think I would ever get married again if she died and that people should only marry once. At the time she said, "You mean if something happens to you and you die, you don't think I should get married? What if we're young and we have kids, you want me to be alone the rest of my life?" She was clear with me that it wasn't an issue for her. So I was open to the idea at this point, but I definitely wasn't ready to date again. In fact, the thought of dating made me sick to my stomach. I mean all the nervousness, awkward first dates, uncertainty, break-ups, and the like gave me knots in my stomach. I certainly had the desire for companionship, but I wasn't ready for it. So while I initially passed off the kids' request, I did eventually pray about it, but in a very passive way. "Lord, if You want me to get remarried, I'll be open to it." Over the weeks and months as the kids would ask again, I began to find the whole thing quite funny. I remember one particular day when it came up again. We were driving on the freeway and Augustine said, "Dad, when can we go get a new mom?" I laughed a little at his question, as he made it sound so simple – "go get a new mom."

I asked him, "Son, what do you think, I can just go to a store and pick out a wife?"

He said, "Yes, let's go now." I of course explained that this was not how it worked. We laughed about it and he told me what he wanted in a mom. He described his desired key features, like "long legs and blonde hair." (I'm not making that one up!) Then he said, "Don't worry Dad, I'll find you a new wife."

We opted not to go to the "wife" store that day and we

went on about our days, Gianna in school, Augustine in preschool – though that was not going that well. He went a few times here and there, but he often did not want to leave me. I would work from home and he would play at my feet or in the room next to me. I believe this time was such a grace for us. That I even had the ability to have him with me at my side was a gift.

While I was still not fully clear on what my next stage in life would look like, I did know one thing. I knew I had to finish the book we set out to write before Angela died. Angela had told me before she died to finish the book. She also, as I shared earlier, had said very plainly, "I want the world to know, that no matter what, they must trust in Jesus." I knew in my heart of hearts that this book needed to be written for that very reason.

I began revising the book and decided on changing it quite drastically. I remember my friend and author, Mark Hart, saying to me when Angela was near death, "The last few chapters are being written right in front of us." How right he was! I spent much of the rest of 2012 reading what I had written and reorganizing the book. I had a friend help me organize all of the posts Angela and I had written over the seventeen-month journey into one document and I began organizing the content. That content alone added up to over 70 pages and some 50,000 words. I used this content to help me come up with a new outline and set out to write this book all over again.

As I did this work, I also spoke with several friends who were authors or involved in publishing. One of the big questions I received from them was whether or not I would go out to speak around the country to promote the book. I didn't really know if I wanted to or should. Sure, I was happy to talk about Angela's faith and her journey, but should I? Is that what God wanted for me? So I took it to prayer. The very next day a friend called, asking me if I could come speak in Boston that February and share our testimony. I took this as an answer to my prayer. I said yes, and I began to get a few more speaking requests for the next few months.

The days and weeks of that year went swiftly. Christmas was actually much easier to take than I expected and other than a few moments of sadness when we were putting up our Christmas tree, the kids did really well. New Year's Eve was actually much harder for me than the other holidays. For some reason the thought of entering a new year without Angela crushed me. I felt this overwhelming sense of sadness that night after the kids went to bed. After some tears however, my sadness was replaced with even more joy in what was to come. I began the new year with great hope and great excitement.

I continued my work on the book and continued to discern what God was leading me to do with my life. We began to settle into this 'new normal,' and we were figuring out this new life.

I would eventually finish the book, though it took a lot longer than I had hoped. It was very healing to write down Angela's story and it has been an incredible blessing to hear from readers how her story has impacted so many. I believe in my heart of hearts that her story will continue to touch lives for many years to come.

Still, I knew this was not the only way Angela's story would continue to impact people. There was this idea that had been on my mind since just before Angela's death. I'll have to take you back to Angela's story for a bit to adequately explain.

This idea stemmed from our experience in dealing with

Angela's nutritional needs while she underwent treatment. We knew from her initial diagnosis that her prognosis was grim. While we were never given a specific outlook on how long doctors thought she could live, we knew that barring some miracle she likely would not survive this cancer. We did our best to make sure Angela was eating foods that were nourishing and supportive while she was in treatment and also worked hard to keep her from losing weight.

Despite our best efforts, Angela's weight continued to be an issue of concern. Her weight would improve and then she'd get an infection or something else would come up and she would lose weight again. The breaking point came when, after two hospitalizations for a total of about 20 days in one month, Angela lost nearly 25 pounds. That weight loss led to Angela really struggling with treatment, having very low energy, and it seemed to me that she was going downhill. We were already in the process of getting Angela approved to go to a new cancer center as I mentioned earlier in this book.

We went for our first visit there and we were blown away, most of all, by the approach they took to nutrition. First of all, they had incredible food that was delicious and enjoyable. For two people who loved food, this was an important thing! They also had the nutritionist intricately involved in patient care. We knew this was the place for us. Early on, the head of nutrition pulled me aside and let me know that if we didn't get Angela gaining weight, she was in danger of being too underweight to handle treatment. They began to get aggressive with treating her nutrition issues. Because the food was so delicious, chemotherapy days became like dates for us as we ate delicious meals and actually looked forward to going there just for the food! Also, it seemed that Angela did better with her treatments when she was well fed during chemotherapy. She handled the days after chemotherapy better and was able to still eat. This, along with a feeding tube, made all the difference in Angela as she began to put on more weight and have energy again. She also began to see great results from her treatments and we were hopeful that she'd have some more time. The best part of it all was that with the added energy and strength, Angela was able to spend more time enjoying life with our children.

Though Angela eventually succumbed to the disease, we felt so grateful to have had extra time that surely would not have been possible without having gained back some of the weight she had lost and getting the proper nutrition she needed.

Angela shared a couple statistics with me when she was ill: 85% of cancer patients suffer from malnutrition, and 40% of cancer patients actually die from causes related to malnutrition. These facts shocked us both and were a big part of our added effort in regards to her nutrition. These facts were also the impetus behind this idea that had been burning in my mind. The idea actually came when we were leaving the cancer center and taking Angela home for hospice care. I shared earlier how I had spent time on that last day at the hospital saying goodbye to many of the staff we had come to know. One person we said goodbye to was the chef who had been preparing all this incredible food. As I was saying goodbye to him a woman walked by with a large bag filled with to-go meals. The chef explained to me that several patients had started coming for treatment and taking meals home with them to eat in between visits because they couldn't cook this way for themselves.

I left with an idea. What if I opened a kitchen where we prepared nutritious meals for cancer patients and delivered them right to their doors? What if we could serve people nationwide who had cancer and get them the food that would help sustain them during disease?

As I drove Angela home that afternoon, I shared the idea with her. She gave me a big smile and said, "This is your best idea yet. I wish I could be there to see you do it." Looking back, it was as if she knew this was more than an idea. Perhaps she had a glimpse of what was to come.

I didn't really speak of this idea or concept to anyone immediately. I only told Angela and my friend, Dr. John Oertle. He immediately loved the concept, and given his experience, felt it was a much-needed service. He would often bring it up and tell me about different patients of his whom he thought would benefit. I would occasionally dream up ideas of how the business would work, but didn't really feel it was a project I could tackle. I had a background in restaurant management and concept development and was a pretty good home chef. However, it seemed too big of a project and I felt I lacked the financial resources to take it on.

That spring of 2013, as I worked on finishing the book and continually thought about what was next, I spent more and more time on this idea. I began drawing up business models and talking with Dr. Oertle about what was needed for patients. I read and researched a lot about nutrition, and with Dr. Oertle's help, honed in on what we felt was most needed for patients. I began putting the business plan onto paper – including the pricing structure, a budget, and the like. That spring I set my sites on turning this idea into a reality. I didn't launch it immediately, as I was still heavily

IT IS WELL - LIFE IN THE STORM

focused on the book and spending a good deal of time traveling and speaking, but I was certain I would one day start this company.

A NEW LOVE STORY

You remember, of course, that my kids had been asking me about having a new mom. I had promised them that I'd pray and while I was reluctant, I did pray for God to show me if this was His plan for me and to open my heart if it was.

That spring I felt like I was experiencing this expansion of myself. I desired to love another, to give of myself again in that same way I gave of myself to Angela. Not only did I long for that kind of love again, but also felt I was meant for this love, that I was not meant to remain alone. I was hopeful that I would once again experience the joy of marriage. I began to wonder what it would be like to love again. I began to feel hopeful that I could again experience the love that I was missing. There was one reservation that played in my mind. I would often wonder and ask God, "Am I supposed to remain single and take care of our children?" I even thought of one of our favorite Saints, St. Gianna. She died leaving her husband, Pietro, and four young children, including a newborn. Pietro never remarried, dedicating his life to the upbringing of his children. I wondered if that was my calling as well.

As this desire continued I still had one request of God. "Lord, if this is what You want for me, please make it easy. Please let her fall into my lap." I had no desire to go through the many ups and downs of dating. Not only did I not have the free time for such endeavors, the thought of dating made me cringe. So, I made a deal

178

with God, "You make it easy and I'll be open."

Going about dating in my early thirties was foreign and strange for me. I didn't really put a whole lot of effort into it. One night however, after talking with some friends about being open to finding love again, I decided to check out a dating site. I put up a small amount of information about myself so that people wouldn't recognize me and was able to browse the site. The site I was on was particularly for Catholics, and I was actually surprised by the amount of women on the site that I already knew in one way or another. I wondered if they could see my profile too and got a little embarrassed. I didn't immediately go back to the site or set up a full account. Then one day I went back, but this time with the intention of actually putting up some of my information and more intently considering this whole online dating world. I chatted with a few women from the site, but wasn't incredibly intrigued, save one profile of an old friend of mine. Her name was Jennifer and we knew each other in high school through our church. She became a close friend of mine later on in life. We had actually become pretty close in our twenties and spent a lot of time together. We had several mutual friends. For one reason or another we had stopped spending as much time together shortly before I met and started dating Angela. We didn't really keep in touch, but I would hear about her from mutual friends and of course, I would see what she was up to via Facebook. Jennifer had prayed for our family during Angela's cancer journey and even came to Angela's funeral. Seeing her on this site had made me wonder why Jennifer and I never dated. My interest was peaked as I thought about how great a person I knew Jennifer to be.

I decided to say hi via a quick message. Jen responded

and asked how I was, and we exchanged a few messages. Finally I suggested we get together to catch up. With that we made plans for coffee and met one Thursday afternoon in July. We sat for coffee at 3 pm and didn't leave until after 6 pm. We had so many things to catch up on. By the end of our coffee date I only wished it could continue into dinner. Jennifer was just as enjoyable to be with as I remembered. The next day I called her and asked if she'd like to meet up for drinks sometime. We set a date for the following Friday. I took her to a nice restaurant, and we sat at the bar. My thinking was that since we had a previous friendship it would be a good idea to keep it a little casual. Again, we had a great time and an in-depth conversation as we caught up on each other's lives. If it weren't for the obnoxious woman at the bar who began yelling at us halfway through dinner - telling us to loosen up - it was a perfect first date. We left the restaurant and walked for a bit. It was clear to me that I should pursue dating Jennifer and see if there was more than just friendship. We saw each other a couple more times and I then told her my intentions. She was feeling the same but wanted to be sure. Obviously there was a whole different dynamic with me being a recent widower with children and she needed to process, and so did I. We had a long conversation one night and talked through various reservations and the dynamics of a potential relationship. Jennifer found peace with it all and we continued our courtship. The discernment continued, though we both felt very confident that God was leading this.

I still had that thought in the back of my mind of whether or not I was to be like Pietro Molla and simply live the rest of my life single and caring for my children. I asked God for clarity while I began dating Jennifer. That clarity came quite quickly. A deacon from our parish had lost his wife. He and his wife were actually the first people, outside of family, that I saw the day Angela died. He served at the altar for Angela's vigil and funeral. Now it was his wife who passed, and I was there for her funeral. At the end of the Mass, he got up to say a few words. He spoke some beautiful words of his beloved. Then he looked at all of us gathered there and said, "I am yours now. I belong to you." Permanent deacons in the Church can be married, so long as they marry before they are ordained. However, once their spouse dies, they are to be celibate and not remarry. Deacons, like priests, are then fully dedicated to Christ and His Church. As he spoke those words, I felt as though God whispered, "This is not your call."

From that point forward I knew that I should not keep looking back and wondering if I should stay single. Just as I had asked, the Lord had provided, putting Jennifer right in front of me. Not only that, the fact that Jennifer and I had been friends really helped in that there was a comfort level that normally takes a long time to cultivate. We were very honest with each other about our feelings, desires, and intentions for our relationship. It didn't take very long for us to talk about marriage.

Jennifer was such a blessing and a sure sign of God's faithfulness. I was so amazed as over and over God confirmed for us that this was His plan for our lives. One such confirmation came from my son. I had introduced the kids to Jennifer as a friend of mine. They had only been around her about four times when one night, after I got off the phone with Jennifer, Augustine asked, "Dad, was that Jen?"

"Yes," I replied.

"Dad, I think she's going to be my new mom."

A bit surprised by this, I asked, "Really Augustine, why is that?"

"Well, ever since the first time I met her, I just loved her so much."

"Well, I guess we'll see about that," I responded.

"I told you I'd find you a wife, Dad."

It would still be a few weeks before I told the kids I was dating Jennifer, but that little confirmation from Augustine sure did help my discernment.

We continued dating with our eyes on marriage and that December, with my children at my side, I asked Jennifer to be my wife.

God continued to confirm for me that this was the path for our family. There was one such confirmation that came in a subtle but profound way. I have long had a devotion to Saint Therese and had prayed a Saint Therese Novena four times specifically for intercession in regards to whether or not I should remarry and also in finding a wife. One day, while Jennifer and I were dating I found a St. Therese Novena card that was specifically asking St. Therese for a rose. Many people tell stories of St. Therese sending them roses as signs of answered prayers. I said that prayer in a simple fashion and asked St. Therese for a rose as a confirmation. A few days later I was talking with Jennifer when I realized I never knew her middle name. I asked her and she replied, "Rose." I didn't even make the connection right then, but the very next day it hit me. The confirmation I sought came in her very name.

We were married at Our Lady of Mount Carmel Catholic Church in May of the following year. As we prepared for our marriage we were keenly aware of the fact that marriage is at one time joyous and full of sacrifices. We wanted our wedding to be a witness to this fact. The night before our wedding I gave Jennifer the following note with the crucifix I gave her as her wedding gift.

Dear Jen,

There is a story of a town in Europe that has zero divorce. Why? Because they understand that at the heart of marriage is the cross. In their wedding Mass, the couple places their hands on the crucifix and commits to "take up their cross" together.

Life and death, they're both before us. I promise to take up the cross with you at all times. St. Francis used to say to his friars, "Let us begin..." So I say to you my love, let us begin this journey and bear our crosses as one.

Love,
Chris

I spoke with Father John Bonavitacola, who was set to marry us, about this and asked him if he was familiar with this practice of placing the hands on the crucifix. He was familiar with the practice, which he said was frequent in many Eastern Rite Catholic Churches and agreed to include a version in our Mass. He simply told me that he'd have something written down for me to say. After we said our vows, Father John handed us the crucifix I had given Jennifer the night before and blessed it. We placed our hands over the Crucifix and he handed me a small card with a prayer on it for me to read. "Jennifer, may God who has revealed

His glory to us in Christ, bring our married life into conformity with the image of His Son, so that we may reach the vision of His glory."

With our vows spoken and those simple words of seeking conformity with Christ crucified and Christ risen, we, as St. Francis and so many Saints after him oft said, set out to "begin again."

I'm constantly amazed at the love God has given me in Jennifer. As I put that ring on her finger, a new journey began. Our faith informs us that when a man and woman are married, they become a new creation. The old self dies and a new creation rises – two distinct people in union with the other, in communion with the other through the Triune God. We become new and are made in the image and likeness of the Trinity. The old self doesn't cease to exist, of course. We bring into our marriage our history, our past, our experiences, our family, and often times some baggage. I brought two children into this marriage. I also brought to it the fond memory and legacy of Angela. I brought with me the mission God placed in front of me – to share His message through Angela's story and to help people suffer well. Jennifer has been gracious in encouraging us to remember Angela and to keep her memory alive in our home. She has been there to comfort our children when they miss their "Mom in heaven," as they call her. She has painstakingly sorted through and archived memories and pictures of Angela and is even putting together memory boxes and scrapbooks for both Gianna and Augustine of their mother. She has been a supportive partner in this mission and work God has called me to do.

Jennifer and I both desired more children and prayed that God would bless us with more. We got pregnant shortly after our wedding and were overjoyed with the prospect of a new child. It seemed that life couldn't get any better. We were living a dream come true. Every day we got more and more excited about this new life coming our way. Jennifer began to show signs that we might lose the baby. We were only eleven weeks pregnant, but this new life seemed to be coming to an end. Jennifer had a painful miscarriage – both physically and emotionally. They don't tell you that miscarriage can be like a "mini-birth." The contractions were grueling and all the while we knew what they meant. This little baby was a sign of hope and now she was a reminder that life is fragile and often times painful. We lost her on August 17, 2014, less than three months after our wedding. We were blessed that our diocese has a burial program for miscarried babies born earlier than twenty weeks. We named her Sophia Grace and we buried her in the same cemetery Angela was buried in, a short two years earlier. Heartache set in and we faced a new suffering in our home. God was faithful as always and brought us through in beautiful ways. Jennifer exhibited such faith, despite a deep heartache.

As we healed from that new loss, we grew in faith and our resolve to trust in God. Now, we had two members of our family in heaven praying for us. This loss also opened old wounds; our daughter, Gianna, began to experience more grief and sadness over her mother. Many of the things she didn't express or seem to experience immediately after Angela's death surfaced, and our family now worked through this grief together. I recall one night with Gianna where I was struggling to calm her and comfort her. I finally asked if she'd want to talk to her mom (Jennifer) about it. She did and afterward said she felt a lot better, with a smile on her face. The kids went through a grief program, which seemed to help

Gianna.

A few months after our miscarriage, Jennifer and I were ready to try again. We conceived and in August of 2015, we welcomed Maximilian Jude to our family. He has been a true joy for all of us. His life is a gift and our world will never be the same.

ALL THINGS WORK FOR GOOD

After working for a couple of years on my business idea to serve the chronically ill with nutrient-rich foods to sustain them during disease, Jennifer and I, along with three business partners, decided to launch Bene Plates. My time researching and planning this business proved to me there is a profound need for a service such as ours. Cancer patients need our food. People with other chronic illnesses, who are also prone to malnutrition and other nutrition deficiencies, need our food as well.

Our model is to prepare meals weekly and ship them to our clients' homes across the country. The meals are made with sustainably raised and grown ingredients, geared at ensuring a high micronutrient content full of great flavor and aimed at helping our clients with various taste issues. We also provide a nutrition component. A staff nutritionist is able to evaluate and consult with our clients to ensure they are getting optimum nutrition during their disease.

In October 2015 we launched with a crowd-funding campaign on Kickstarter.com. Crowd funding gives companies a way to launch their product through pre-orders. Our goal for our Kickstarter campaign was simply to raise awareness about our product. It gave us a great way to get the word out and gain a few early customers who provided valuable feedback to help us improve our program.

I'm happy to say that we are now serving customers nationwide and providing a valuable service that is helping people in a profound way. I've been so blessed to hear from people about how they are benefiting from our food. One physician we work with shared with me that one of his patients who was receiving our meals was in tears when sharing with him how much she was eating. She thought she might never be able to eat again. When we met her, she could barely eat a few bites of a meal. About a month later, when sharing this with her physician, she was eating more than half of a meal.

We are seeing some wonderful results like this with many clients, and we are so blessed to work with these families. Often times, the person we are actually interacting with is the caregiver. I'm finding that supporting the caregivers is a major part of our work. These people are pouring out blood, sweat, and tears to love and care for their spouse, parent, sibling, child, or friend with whatever illness they are facing. Often times they are overwhelmed and beleaguered by the task at hand. Studies show that with some chronic illnesses the caregiver is at risk of health issues of their own, due to the incredible stress they face every second of the day. Statistics show that approximately 1/3 of caregivers of those with Alzheimer's Dementia die before the patient.

With this in mind, our focus has increasingly been on supporting the caregiver to give the best possible care they can, while reducing their stress. One of our clients is a sweet wife and mother. Her husband has advanced cancer and she was working very diligently to support him. She had been reading every book she could, taking nutrition advice from many people, and spending hours a day making her husband food that she felt would support his healing. Our team was able to support her by providing dinners that are harder for her to make. She still makes smoothies and breakfasts for him, but she tells me that the reduced amount of work has really helped her. It is very rewarding to support not only her husband, but support her as well. Having been the caregiver, I identify with what these people go through every single day as they sacrifice parts of their lives to support the ones they love. Every day Bene Plates is growing and learning what it means to care for our clients.

We also have many clients who are just regular folks without any chronic illnesses who want to eat healthy for general wellness. Many of them have chosen our company so they can come alongside us in our mission to serve the chronically ill. We are not alone in our mission.

As life goes on for us down here, I see now how God certainly makes good of all things for those who love him. I see so clearly now what Angela understood at the end. She understood that her death was not in vain and that so much fruit would come of her suffering and our loss. As we move forward in this new mission, I see now that God was again preparing us for what was to come.

Everything in life, the good, the bad, the extreme high points of joy and bliss, along with the downright awful pain and difficulty of loss or failure – all of it is ordered to get us to heaven. And all of it, all along the way is ordered to make us into the beings God created us to be. All of it, the good and the bad, is geared to getting each of us to the next step on our journey. For our family, the journey of life on this earth was not over – but for Angela, this part of her journey was over, and it was time for the next. What were we here below to do? Wait in lament for heaven? No, that is not God's desire for any of us. He does not ask us to simply bide our time on this earth in wait for heaven. God gave each of us life and wants us to have it abundantly (John 10:10). Angela went on to live the life she always dreamed of, and while we await our time to live that same life, we have chosen as a family to live abundantly with joy. By God's grace, we chose to take this sour and awful experience and allow God to make it good by serving others, by allowing new love into our life, and allowing new life to be born.

I pray for you, that you, too, will choose to allow God to make good of all things in your own life. If there is any one thing I think Angela would have wanted her life to testify to, it is that favorite scripture of hers, Romans 8:28, "We know all things work for good for those who love God, who are called according to His purpose."

About the Author

Chris Faddis is a dedicated husband and father, speaker, author,
and entrepreneur. He has a diverse
background in church ministry,
marketing, and restaurant management and development. Since
the death of his first wife, Angela,
he has devoted his time to writing,
speaking, and creating sustain-
able business models to serve the

healthcare needs of the chronically ill. Chris is a regular guest on
television and radio programs sharing his story along with offering insight on healthcare and end of life issues. He is remarried
to Jennifer, and together they raise their three children, Gianna,
Augustine, and Maximilian, in Chandler, Arizona. Chris is the
founder of Bene Plates, a food and nutrition company that pro-
vides high quality nutrition to the chronically ill and the walking
well. Chris has also founded the Angela Faddis Fund to support
those who are chronically ill and cannot afford proper nutrition.

MEDIA AND SPEAKING REQUESTS

Chris Faddis is available to speak to church groups, businesses, cancer advocacy groups, and palliative care organizations.

Contact: media@beneplates.com

BENE PLATES

For more information about our nutrition and meal delivery programs, inlcuding pricing and menus, visit or call:

www.beneplates.com | 480-459-3334

THE ANGELA FADDIS FUND

A donor advised fund has been set up in memory of Angela Faddis at the Catholic Community Foundation of Phoenix. This fund is dedicated to supporting healthcare initiatives - with a primary focus on helping to fund meals and nutrition services for clients who are unable to afford these services.

To make a tax-deductible donation online or by mail:

www.ccfphx.org/donate
1. Click the "Donor Advised Fund" tab
2. Select "Angela Faddis Fund"

Catholic Community Foundation
400 East Monroe Street
Phoenix, AZ 85004
1. Please make checks payable to the "Catholic Community Foundation"
2. Write "Angela Faddis Fund" in the memo section

CPSIA information can be obtained
at www.ICGtesting.com
Printed in the USA
BVHW091243221220
596051BV00006B/15